GREEK
LYRIC
POETRY

A New Translation

SHEROD
SANTOS

W. W. NORTON & COMPANY

New York   London

Excerpt from *Autumn Journal* by Louis MacNeice, published by Faber & Faber Ltd.,
is reprinted with permission of David Higham Associates Ltd.

For information about permission to reproduce selections
from this book, write to Permissions, W. W. Norton & Company, Inc.,
500 Fifth Avenue, New York, NY 10110

Manufacturing by Courier Westford
Book design by JAM Design
Production manager: Anna Oler

Library of Congress Cataloging-in-Publication Data

Greek lyric poetry : a new translation / Sherod Santos.— 1st ed.
p. cm.
Includes bibliographical references and index.
ISBN 0-393-06056-X (hardcover)
1. Greek poetry—Translations into English. I. Santos, Sherod, 1948–
PA3622.S26 2005
884'.0108—dc22

2005018032

W. W. Norton & Company, Inc., 500 Fifth Avenue,
New York, N.Y. 10110
www.wwnorton.com

W. W. Norton & Company Ltd. Castle House,
75/76 Wells Street, London W1T 3QT

1 2 3 4 5 6 7 8 9 0

for Lynne

CONTENTS

ACKNOWLEDGMENTS

Because I've allowed myself varying degrees of license with these translations—degrees, at times, classicists are rightly inclined to resist—I wish to both thank and release from responsibility Professors Raymond Marks and David Schenker from the Department of Classical Studies at the University of Missouri-Columbia. Their keen scholarly minds have added greatly to my understanding of the period, and their detailed annotations, queries, and suggested alternatives to late drafts of the manuscript have saved me from blunders in tone and fact. The slow burn of a Highland malt seems scant reward for their labors.

I've also benefited from the sure-handed poetic insights of Lynne McMahon, Bryan Narendorf, and Averill Curdy, and from the ungrudging counsel of Rosanna Warren, whose passionate belief in the art of translation has been a source of inspiration from the start. Lastly, I feel quite sure that the ever-rising tide of transcripts, reprints, notes, and revisions would've swamped me early on had it not been for the assistance of my beloved coworkers, past and present: Sharon Fisher, Brian Barker, and Bob Watts.

Without the touch of all their hands, this book would be a more stumbling and haphazard thing.

Grateful acknowledgment is also made to the editors of the following journals, in which many of these poems first appeared: *Poetry, Raritan, Slate, The Georgia Review, The Gettysburg Review, Literary Imagination, Parnassus: Poetry in Review, Smartish Pace, Washington Square, Margie: The American Journal of Poetry, Tiferet, Redbud*. An abbreviated version of the Introduction also first appeared in *Raritan*.

INTRODUCTION

Someone, I tell you, will remember us,
even in another time
                —Sappho (fr. 147)

These dead are dead . . .
And how can one imagine oneself among them
        I do not know;
It was all so unimaginably different
        And all so long ago.
            —Louis MacNeice, *Autumn Journal*

We are born with the dead:
See, they return, and bring us with them.
            —T. S. Eliot, "Little Gidding"

lyre, lyre, lyre
                —Sappho (fr. 176)

"The only true motive for putting poetry into a fresh language," Dante Gabriel Rossetti wrote in his introduction to *The Early Italian Poets*, "must be to endow a fresh nation, as far as possible, with one more possession of beauty." My primary aim in translating these poets has been to assist in that endowment, to help make some space for the pleasures of a poetry that continues to speak both passionately and clearly to our shared experiences of boredom, dread, wonder, happiness, the shadows on our pillows, the longings in our hearts, the whole frazzled, ragtag welter of particulars that make up a human life. As such, the collection is addressed to the general reader, to poets and lovers of poetry, to those who might be coming to these poems for the very first time, and perhaps as well to professional Hellenists who are curious about the slips and recombinations that occur when poets in the present attempt to commune with poets in the past.

I have gathered here what contemporary readers will recognize as a collection of "lyric" poems, though that term is accurate only in a loose and relatively recent sense. Given their habit of changing through time, genre distinctions are notoriously difficult to pin down, and this is especially true in the case of the lyric. While the term denotes, in the modern age, a specific set of formal, expressive, even tonal concerns, it's far less explicit when applied to antiquity, where it referred, more simply, to any poetry that was sung. What we call a "lyric" today, the ancients came to call an "epigram" (whose primary meaning was "inscription"), and within that tradition distinctions of genre were often made, not by the poem's metrical properties—epic by dactylic hexameter, elegy by the elegiac couplet, lyric (typically) by the choriamb—but by the accompanying musical instrument. Epic, for example, was chanted to the deep, resounding tones of the *cithara* (a stringed instrument with a box-shaped resonator, similar to but larger than the lyre), whereas elegy was accompanied on the pipe, and lyric sung to the lyre (though occasionally the oboe-like *aulos* would serve in its place).

Still, while it seems clear that the poets of the Archaic and Classical Periods performed their poems to the accompaniment of musical instruments, this practice grew less common in the Hellenistic and Roman Periods as the written word took on increasingly greater importance in both the composition and reception of poetry. By the time of Horace, the shift from an oral to a literate tradition was already well underway; poetic devices such as the acrostic began to appear, as did "inaudible" verse forms like *isopsepha*, wherein the sum of letters in each couplet adds up to the same number. Poems were beginning to make their appeal to the eye as well as to the ear, and this shift in emphasis would soon become an integral part of a poem's reception. In the Roman and Early Byzantine Periods, the oral/aural beginnings of poetry had developed into a semi-oral/semiliterate tradition.

All of that said, I'll hereafter employ the term "lyric" in its more modern sense, with the understanding, first, that the term includes such forms as elegy, iambus, and epigram (thereby marking it a categorical alternative to the epic), and, second, that in the overall span of this collection the oral character of ancient poetry was central to its appreciation.

So where do these poems come from? And how did they come to be what they are? Although we have no historical record to document its development, it seems clear that the lyric as we know it today was born and came to maturity in the time between the epic of Homer and the Latin poetry of the Republic—roughly, from the seventh through the first century B.C. Indeed, since those poems were written after Homer and before Horace and Catullus, one might trace their evolution by noting how far they depart from the former, and how closely they anticipate the latter, an evolution that occurs, in the gene pool of poetry's forms and characteristics, with the raw, adaptive purposes of a Darwinian model.

While the growth of this form has always induced a special kind of fascination in me, the thought of attempting versions of my own arose only by happenstance. A chance encounter with a fragment of Sappho's led me to track down, in our university's cavernous library stacks, a handful of English translations; and those, in turn, led me back to the originals in J. M. Edmonds' *Lyra Graeca*, a three-volume edition containing early Greek sources along with en face plain prose trots—the Virgilian guide to those of us who have little or no Greek save that received through translation.

What remains of Sappho's oeuvre appears in the first of those volumes, and the library's copy, published in 1922, was bruised and weathered from age, broken at the spine, its bilious green covers held together by two oversize rubber bands. It was early winter, a drear season in the Midwestern Plains, and while sitting at a table in the library's dim-lit reading room, I pored over each of the 192 fragments, often no more than a single contextless word or phrase ("because of my pain" is one such entry, "wrapped her all about with soft cambric" is another), some recovered from lacunose scraps of

Egyptian papyri, others handed down in the form of citations by later writers, historians, scholiasts, and grammarians. So as not to further strain the binding, I cushioned Edmonds' book against my overcoat, though no matter how carefully I turned the pages, tiny bits of yellowing paper flaked off onto the table. I'm not sure why, but reading Sappho under those conditions—the raw winter sunlight draining off the room's high windows, the pages moldering before my eyes—affected me in ways I find difficult to explain. Difficult, perhaps, because the effect combined contrary feelings for their remoteness in time and their nearness in spirit: a sharp sense of the fleeting presence of human life, and the enduring if still melancholy fact that my reading somehow fulfilled the promise a Lesbian poet made centuries ago: "Someone, I tell you, will remember us."

To read Sappho is to gaze across the ever-widening gulf of history into the flickering lucidities of an interior life, a scattered dialogue of self and soul that seems to begin where Penelope left off, in a brooding meditation on love and loss—the anguish of separation, the intense carnality of the loved one's presence, the rattled, nerve end wait for love's return—all the keen desiderata of a heart ensconced dead center in the sway of any given moment. This is all the more remarkable when we stop to consider that, in Sappho's work, the historical preeminence of myth, with its warring gods and godlike heroes, is quietly supplanted by a human voice, a woman's voice speaking to the concerns of her daily life, a solitary daring to posit the notion that the ordinary experience of human love is imbued with significance as worthy of attention as all the martial splendors of Homerica. And out of this seemingly plain ambition is born a poetry that becomes the site for a radical shift in our cultural conceptions of self and other, and in the language by which the conventions of human relations are formed.

Of course, Sappho was not alone in readjusting the protocols of poetry, however indelibly she marked their course. And reading through the work of other poets from the period, I realized that, to a large extent, what I felt that afternoon was connected in turn to the affective nature of the lyric poem, to the sheer romance of reading verses composed at the dawn of that lapidary, inward-looking form. A form through which the human figure, brought out from the shadow of heroes and gods, rises to its true, unexalted height. A form where language is duly released from its functional role as a conveyance for meaning, narrative, fact, to assume, instead, a lighter, more aerial spirit, like the feathery play of sensation.

One can't help feel elated at being privy to an era of such bold inventiveness and rampant artistic intuition; and that elation helps explain why Romantic Hellenists from Winckelmann and Hölderlin to Byron and Nietzsche returned to it as a countermodel to the stifling bourgeois culture. Moreover, my reading made me all the more aware of how indebted we are to the long and distinguished line of scholars who, with the painstaking care of an archaeological dig, have made available not only a reliable set of prose translations, but also the lavishly annotated remains of the originals.

At the same time, my reading left me with the impression that, with notable periodic exceptions, the originals aren't always so well represented on the poetic side of things, that all too often the translations remain, as Shakespeare put it, "tongue-tied by authority." Perhaps the canonical status of classical literature awakens in us an instinctual reluctance to tamper, as though any divergence from the literal marked a kind of desecration, a despoiling of something time has set off as sacred ground. (A derivative of the Latin *classicus,* "classical" originally signified "of the highest class of Roman citizen," hence the antiquarian basis for its modern connections to social class.) And perhaps that deference tempts us into the binary trap of thinking about translation in either/or terms: scholarly/poetic, literal/literary, faithful/unfaithful. But such oppositions fail to acknowledge how interactive the two sides are; more important, they fail to acknowledge how essential that interaction is to the continued life of our literary past.

"Without scholarship," wrote the distinguished classicist D. S. Carne-Ross, "no classical text could survive and be read, but scholarship alone cannot preserve a poet as a vital presence. That is the task of poets and good readers of poetry from generation to generation." The fact that, apart from Sappho, the poets in this collection are largely unknown and little read by anyone other than specialists in the field, may point, in part, to that problem. While scholars have preserved their linguistic record and historical traces, literary translators (in English, at least) have been far less resolute about maintaining their "vital presence," that fire whereby our language is stamped, as Horace remarked, with "the mint-mark of the day."

In the ideal and colossal library that Jorge Luis Borges carried around in his head, all thinkers and poets were contemporary, their ideas and songs were endlessly brought forward into the modern idiom, their insights, quandaries, joys, and pains were endlessly reexperienced in the here and now. Such faith in the verity of literature "stands for something brave," he said, "stands for the idea that one *believes* in philosophy or that one *believes* in poetry—that things beautiful once can go on being beautiful still." If my interest in Greek poetry has taught me anything, it's that we have good reason to maintain our belief in its livable charms, and to uphold our faith that the animated life it once possessed is no less germane to our lives now. Of course, how a translation rekindles that life is a matter of great debate, especially in the case of poetry, where one is drawn to outreach its literal meanings in order to secure some sense of its aesthetic, expressive, and phonic appeal. This necessity requires that I say a few things about the translation methods I've adopted.

In an Attic vase picture, *c.* 430 B.C., Sappho holds a book on which is written, "The words I begin are words of air, but, for all of that, good to hear." That sentence has remained tacked above my work desk as a kind of instructive riddle. For however much things would change in time, the lyric begins in an age when Greeks had little use for written texts, preferring the live and mutable nature of the spoken word over the fixed, inalterable nature of the written; that is, preferring words that pass from throat-to-ear over those that pass from hand-to-eye. I've therefore taken Sappho's sentence as a kind of license to think of the originals as formed from "words of air"—that is, from sounds—and to seek out sounds in the English language that make them, likewise, "good to hear." Not proper translations, in the strict sense, but not exactly imitations or paraphrases or verse transfers either. I suppose I think of them as collaborations, for while they're firmly grounded in poems composed more than two thousand years ago—and wholly dependent on the scholarship from those intervening years—they still tend toward a kind of self-sufficiency, or at least toward a kind of felicity that comes from pursuing more the tonal than the denotative meanings of the originals. In the end, this seemed faithful to the live, extempore spirit of an oral tradition, faithful, as well, to the special value the ancients assigned to the simple pleasures of hearing a poem. To evoke rather than to mimic has been my general rule.

While these "translation choices" reflect priorities of my own, they also reflect necessities born of linguistic and cultural differences between ancient Greek and modern English. The early Greeks made no distinction between poetry and song. Their poems were meant to be memorized and recited and improvised, and listeners might actually tap their feet to maintain the beat of the music. And because they were composed to be heard and not read, typographical practices that are givens today—line breaks, punctuation, initial capitalization, and so on—did not exist in the original papyrus. There the words were run together in columns of unpunctuated uppercase letters, and such things as stanzaic shapes were only determined by later scholarship on the basis of measures appropriate to the poem's music. Any "visual" replication of the original would render it unintelligible to today's reader.

Likewise, re-creating in English the metrical forms of the originals would only muddle the stripped-down naturalness of expression that is a hallmark of these poems. Such an effort might well be admired for its ingenuity—as in the eccentric attempt of Louis and Celia Zukofsky to render Catullus by finding English words that come closest to reproducing the sounds of the original Latin—but since the two languages possess such different phonic qualities,

English versions of Greek meters can hardly come close to approximating the "music" of the original. Greek words, for instance, don't possess the stress accents so defining of English; accordingly, the ancient poets fashioned their measures around the time it took to pronounce the different syllables, and they formed their lines from a pattern made by combining syllables of different duration. As Greek scholars remind us, English-speakers tend to misread Greek poetry because we naturally stress the syllables that take the downbeat, while the early Greeks found the sweep of their rhythm in the duration of the syllables alone.

Still, in my original free verse sketches, as I tried to gauge the tone that seemed truest to my ear, I ended up feeling that something was missing, that sense of the made thing that forms such a bracing counterpoint to the day-to-day concerns of these poems. Accordingly, I've chosen to work in a variety of meters and stanzaic shapes, some with Greek roots, some without—decasyllabic couplets, elegiac stanzas, sapphics, accentuals, free verse, even, on one or two occasions, forms as remote as renga and haiku—though my stock-in-trade has remained the commonest English measure, the blank verse line.

On the whole I've avoided the practice of employing for effect archaic terms and phrasings (a practice that can often seem like the fad for "antiquing" new furniture), or of peppering the language with modern slang (like the fad for painting antique furniture so it appears to be new). Instead, I've opted for the grainy surfaces of unfinished wood, the rough pitch and raw materiality of the original. I've also sought to present these pieces disencumbered of the usual scholarly annotations that broad historical transmissions normally entail. Rather, I've limited my notes to points of biographical, historical, or literary interest; or, to put it more plainly, to information that has added to my own enjoyment of the poems.

As with most issues involved in translating the ancients, translators are divided in their approaches to the transliteration of Greek proper names. Does one preserve the distinction between those poets with Greek names who were living in the Greek-speaking world and those poets with Roman names and of Roman birth who wrote in Greek? In almost all cases I have opted for the familiar (writing Plato, for example, instead of Platon), which means that I've employed the traditional anglicized (romanized) spellings. I've followed a similar instinct in attaching titles to poems. The Greeks did not use titles—this is largely a modern phenomenon—and where they do exist copyists or other authors appended them. But the modern reader is accustomed to the grounding a title can provide, and I've often found a title can illuminate a poem that is otherwise opaque.

As mentioned, many of the pieces I've included derive from scraps of papyrus, while others derive from citations embedded in the texts of other authors. I decided against the practice of inserting ellipses to indicate lacunae or providing commentary to outline the history of the scholarly debate surrounding those missing passages. On occasion, I've taken the liberty of juxtaposing particular fragments in such a way that they invite connections that couldn't have existed otherwise, my sole defense being that the whole seemed somehow emotionally richer than the sum of its parts. Still, scholars determined to keep "incomplete" texts housebound in their scholarly trappings complain about those who present a fragment as though it were "a poem," and I will no doubt provide them with further irritation. But I don't insist on presenting the fragments as poems, which they may or may not be, so much as poetry, which, to my mind, all of the ones I've selected are. And if some of those fragments appear to take on the wholeness of a poem, then perhaps that simply tells us something about the mystery and obliquity of lyric poetry.

For general reference, I've provided a century for each author in the Contents, though of course some poets cross over centuries, and, for others, chronographers differ or are uncertain.

If we think of poetic forms as shapes for particular kinds of thought, and of new poetic forms as shapes for new possibilities for thought, then the early Greek poems keep the record of a remarkable phenomenon: the manifestation of a new way for people to think about the conditions of their own lives. In Archilochus (seventh century B.C.), for example, we encounter the first poet to construct entire poems around the autobiographical particulars of his own life; and in so doing, he also became the first poet to use the lyric as a vehicle for criticizing the social, political, and military structures of the day. We live in a time when the lyric is often discounted for its supposedly asocial and narcissistic limits, but imagine what it meant for members of a small community to listen to a poet whose poems referred, not to the stock of literary characters, but to the people and social relations and governing structures around them. And who did so in a language that readily employed modern phrasings and idioms. Not only was the lingua franca considered an appropriate vehicle for the transmission of poetry, the poem itself was regarded as a kind of event that continues happening in time, happening in the voices of sailors and street vendors and swineherds and cooks, happening in the wheat fields and marketplaces, in small huts and in the open air.

Of course, in Greek society poetry possessed a significance it no longer possesses today, at least not in the Western world. In the seventh and sixth centuries B.C., poets were regarded as teachers and holy men, more like shamans or medicine men than our artists today. And poetry was still considered the most effective medium for thinking, for working out those stubborn philosophical issues that lie at the core of human life. As Aristotle observed, poetry is better suited for this task than history because history is bound to think about what has already happened, while poetry is free to imagine what might still happen yet. History is bound by what we've been, while poetry can imagine our becomings. *Poiesis,* in the Greek sense, literally meant "creation."

As such, the ancient poets played a more determinate role in the political and social evolution of their society than poets do today. A poet like Solon could be authorized to rewrite Athenian law; a lame schoolmaster like Tyrtaeus could be summoned from Athens to lead the Spartans in the Second Messenian War; Archilochus was called to lead a colony and Simonides to make peace between warring armies. Likewise, writing poetry was not considered the exclusive domain of poets. Even Socrates, who died without leaving any written work behind, was believed to have written a hymn to Apollo and an Aesopian fable in epic verse. In a memorable passage in Plato's *Phaedo,* the elder recalls: "I composed these poems . . . because I wanted to test the meaning of certain dreams I had."

Since we are in some inevitable way a historical and cultural projection (however contested that projection may be) of the meaning the ancient poets dreamed, we might rightly assume we have something to gain by returning to the poems that were their test. We might even find that *what* we gain is something we already possess, something that's already part of us, something as familiar as it is strange. "And the end of all our exploring," as T. S. Eliot observed, "Will be to arrive where we started / And know the place for the first time." In the spirit of that homecoming, my fondest hope is that this book be judged by the degree to which it stimulates an interest in reading that goes well beyond the limits and limitations of its pages, and that it provides some access to the pleasures of a poetry whose yearnings once ardently sang through our blood.

A NOTE ON SOURCES

For my primary sources I've relied on the standard scholarly texts, most particularly the Loeb Classical Library's five-volume edition of *The Greek Anthology* by W. R. Paton; the three-volume edition of *Lyra Graeca* and the two-volume edition of *Elegy and Iambus* by J. M. Edmonds; the five-volume edition of *Greek Lyric* by David A. Campbell; and the single-volume edition of *Greek Elegiac Poetry* by Douglas E. Gerber. I have also consulted texts and commentaries by C. M. Bowra in *Greek Lyric Poetry*, and A. S. F. Gow and D. L. Page in *Hellenistic Epigrams* and *The Garland of Philip*. In fewer instances I've turned to E. Diehl's *Anthologia Lyrica Graeca*, and to D. L. Page's *Poetae Melici Graeci* and *Supplementum Lyricis Graecis*. For those interested in more precise distinctions and more detailed discussions of the metrical issues involved, I recommend three excellent studies: M. L. West's *Greek Metre*, A. H. Sommerstein's *The Sound Pattern of Ancient Greek*, and W. S. Allen's *Accent and Rhythm*. To all of these authors I am deeply indebted.

I

ARCHAIC

AND

CLASSICAL

PERIODS

(c. 700–323 B.C.)

ECLIPSE

Nothing can surprise me now, nothing can astonish
or alarm me now the god of gods has galled the midday
into night and trimmed the light of the westering sun.
Surely anything can happen now, anything at all,
so brace yourselves for the sight of milk cows grazing
the dolphin-crowded seas, of sure-footed deer
and mountain goats crossing the talus of a cresting wave.

Archilochus

PORTENT

Look, Glaucus, the broad-backed combers
are running high, storm clouds black out
Gyrae's peaks, and around my heart
a fear that rises from the unforeseen.

Archilochus

THE RALLYING

No man shall stay sober while on my watch!
So get up now, take this bowl and draw out
draughts from the wooden tuns—
drain them down to their wine-sapped lees—
then pass it around from man to man
along the bench of our trim-beaked ship.

Archilochus

PRAYER

Often by loose, unraveling strands of gray
sea foam, rawboned seamen are rumored to pray
for the long-braided goddess to lead their way.

Archilochus

ABANTIAN WARRIORS

Mark my words, not long bow, javelin,
or slingshot stone will account for the river
of blood that runs when the war god
makes his melee on the plain, but the piked
sword of the crew-cut Abantian warrior
advancing through the mayhem hand to hand.

Archilochus

THE SHIELD

Some half-cocked Thracian swaggers about
raising up before his men my blazoned shield,
the one I abandoned near a blackthorn tree.
So? It's not my head he's ragging them with,
and any old shield can replace that one.

Archilochus

ARETE

Rise up, warriors, take your stand at one another's sides,
your feet set wide and rooted like oaks in the ground.
Then bide your time, biting your lip, for you were born
from the blood of Heracles, unbeatable by mortal men,
and the god of gods has never turned his back on you.

So cast off whatever fears arise at the armored legions
they'll muster before you, hedge yourselves round
with hollow shields, and learn to love death's ink-
black shadow as much as you love the light of dawn.
So that when the hour comes, the battle lines drawn,

you won't hang back beyond javelin and stone but,
marshaled into ranks, advance as one to engage your enemy
hand to hand. Then hefting your bronze-tipped
spears and raking the air with your broadswords,
set foot to foot, battle dress to weaponry,

horsehair crest to polished mail, and—helmet to helmet,
eye to eye—mangle their gear, hack off limbs, lay open
the organs that warm their chests, then beat them down
until the plain runs red with enemy blood and you
still stand, breathlessly gripping your wet sword's hilt.

Tyrtaeus

HYPNOS

The rills and gullies and saddleback hills are sleeping now,
the talus slopes of the mountain are asleep,
and the low scrub thickets, and the riverine glades.
Sleep gathers in the sound of the water's fall,
in the trade winds riffling the coral shoals;
and all four-footed creatures the black earth breeds—
the race of bees, the gathering tribe of broad-winged birds,
the monsters plundering the bloodshot sea—
all are asleep in the depthless conjuring of that sound.

Alcman

AT THE FEAST OF THE BACCHANTS

Often at night beside a torch-lit glade,
while revelers' chants extol the gods,

she'll show up carrying an auric cup
as large as the bucket a shepherd keeps.

She'll then brim that cup with milk
she's drawn from a lioness, and from that milk

she'll make a cheese, unbroken and white,
in the pine-pitch torches' flickering light.

Alcman

KINGFISHER

Now that I've grown feeble with years,
I can't keep pace with this swirl
of young actors and dancing girls
circling from one show to another.

O, if only I were the kingfisher,
carried aloft on the halcyon's wings,
that sea-blue bird's light passenger
kiting the air like a windborne thing.

Alcman

A SONG FOR ASTYMELOISA

With a glance that loosens
    the body, that dissolves
the body like sleep
    or death, that releases

the body's yearnings,
    she answers me only
by lifting up above
    her head a garland of rose

and melilot, a star fall
    through the late night air,
a haloed shoot, a goose's
    down, that comes to pass

in the moistened after-
    scent that follows her.

                    Alcman

TO PRIAPUS

It's to you, great god of gardens, that Potamon
    leaves his billhook, bush harrow, threshing sledge,
a sickle for harvesting artichokes, the thread-
    bare coat that held off both the wind and rain,

his suntanned oxhide weatherproof boots, a wood-nibbed
    dibble for setting sprouts, and the hammerhead
that in the dog days he'd manhandling wield
    to unblock the sluices and irrigate the beds.

Anonymous

THREE FRAGMENTS FOR APHRODITE'S RETURN

. . . when you return from Crete, meet me
at the apple grove, our little temple,
   its leafy altar incensed with
the mineral scent of your soapy hair

              ·

. . . drifted over blue lakewater,
a cool wind empties out the apple trees,
   a cidery, heavy-eyed drowse
spills from the branches and murmuring leaves

              ·

. . . where the pastured warhorse grazes,
the meadow is awash with spring flowers,
   a serried, wind-lapped lake of blues

Sappho

LAMENT

In the same way that, when the sun sets,
    the whey-colored moon appears
and shadows the newly risen stars,

and lights the acres of flowering corn,
    and prickles with dew the half-
blown rose, the thin-necked melilot,

so, too, even as she longs for Atthis,
    Anactoria shines among
Lydian women, her heart heavy

with loss and desire. I know full well
    the hurt she feels, for her night
cries trouble that dividing sea.

                  Sappho

TO ANACTORIA

Some men say it's the sight of ramparts fronted by cavalry,
others that it's a field of foot soldiers closing ranks,
still others claim that the heart thrills to no spectacle more
than a fleet of warships churning the wine-dark waters white.

I say, instead, the presence of what you love is best.
This is easy enough to understand. Even the far-famed,
milk-skinned Helen abandoned a worthy husband
and, without one thought for child or doting parents,

stole away in a deep-sea ship with the destroyer of Troy.
And now that you are gone, Anactoria, I know that power,
know deep down I would rather see your bare feet
on these flagstones, your face reflected in a looking glass,

than I would watch the man-killing chariots of Lydia
or the sun-enameled armor of the hoplites in battle.

Sappho

INVOCATION

As if yoked to twin swans a bronze carriage
    hauled you back aslant the black earth
(the night air winded from its wing-beat rush),

you showed up breathless at my bedroom door
    to ask again, How am I hurt?
What new heartache have I summoned you for?

Sappho

CRICKETS

When the vaulted sun god lights the sky
with broadcast flame, crickets let spill
from beneath their heat-enameled wings a high,
tuned, if not altogether sobering trill.

Sappho

EROS

    Like a headland wind
thrashing through a leafed-out stand
    of oaks, it rises
in the blood, routing the heart's
    hidden affections.

Sappho

CONCERNING A YOUNG WOMAN

Like a blush pippin ripening on its branch,
the top-most branch, the very tip of a branch
the pickers overlooked—if not overlooked,
then at least so high it outreached their hooks.

.

Like wild hyacinth scattered on a mountain course,
their petals trampled as the shepherds pass
working back down through the lowland vales, the burst-
blue water-colored stains now flower in the dirt.

Sappho

THE CONVERSATION

He must feel blooded with the spirit of a god
to sit opposite you and listen, and reply,
to your talk, your laughter, your touching,
breath-held silences. But what I feel, sitting here
and watching you, so stops my heart and binds
my tongue that I can't think what I might say
to breach the aureole around you there.
It's as if someone with flint and stone had sparked
a fire that kindled the flesh along my arms
and smothered me in its smoke-blind rush.
Paler than the summer grass, it seems
I am already dead, or little short of dying.

Sappho

EVENING STAR

You bring back everything the dawn dispersed.
You bring the sheep back to the fold, the roan
to pasture, the spent child to his mother.
You bring the bride to the waiting bridegroom.

Sappho

ELEGY FOR TIMAS

This earthenware urn holds the ash of one
who was brought unmarried to her funeral.
To grieve for her, friends passed around
a filleting knife and lopped off all their curls.

Sappho

DOVES

As for the stock doves' afternoon song—
since it darkens their hearts, their pinions
loosen and their broody wings decline.

Sappho

SIX FRAGMENTS FOR ATTHIS

I loved you, Atthis, years ago,
when my youth was still all flowers
and sighs, and you—you seemed to me
  such a small ungainly girl.

      ·

Can you forget what happened before?

      ·

If so, then I'll remind you how, while lying
beside me, you wove a garland of crocuses

which I then braided into strands of your hair.
And once, when you'd plaited a double necklace

from a hundred blooms, I tied it around
the swanning, sun-licked ring of your neck.

And on more than one occasion (there were two
of them, to be exact), while I looked on, too

silent with adoration to say your name,
you glazed your breasts and arms with oil.

No holy place existed without us then,
no woodland, no dance, no sound.

•

Beyond all hope, I prayed those timeless
days we spent might be made twice as long.

•

I prayed one word: I *want*.

•

Someone, I tell you, will remember us,
even in another time.

Sappho

THE DANCE

The moon rose late,
and the breathless girls,
each taking her place
around the altar.

Sappho

NOCTURNE

Midnight. The moon
has set, and the Pleiades.
The hours pass
and pass, yet still I lie alone.

Sappho

BATTLE TACKLE

The high-roofed hall soon glittered with bronze,
its broad beams hung with cheek-hinged helmets
trimmed in horsehair and boar-bristle plumes.

And along the wall, loose spears stood gathered
in a seafarer's stook, scotched greaves mounted
on wall pegs, and side by side, or heaped in high

embellished piles, the hard-honed, worm-loop-
patterned swords, the hollowed-out shields,
the mass of unbuckled stud belts and tunics.

For in the war god's name, not a scrap of gear
was untended now that we had rallied in blood
and sworn to take up arms against our enemy.

Alcaeus

THE GOD SHIP

Ask yourself, why is it love never raises
its armored god ship to slaughter the lion,
the red-toothed wolf, and yet can't wait
to storm the heart of my affections?

Ask as well, how could it serve to elevate
a god to burn me down in my sleepless bed?
Or, summoned before Zeus in his skied estate,
to esteem the souvenir of my scorched head?

Alcaeus

DOG STAR

Why not wet our lungs with wine, Sirius
is coming on, the dog days are upon us,

streets and alleys warping in the swelter,
cicadas in acacia trees, artichokes in flower.

For now it begins, the drawn-out quarrel
that, mounted in the blood, makes young girls

turn lascivious, and men stand stunned
scalded by the light of the midday sun.

Alcaeus

STORM SEASON

I can't make sense of these offshore winds.
One lumbering comber crests this way,
the next one crests the other,
and in between we're bandied about,
barely afloat in our steep-hulled ship.

A brackish bilge water floods the hold,
day by day a slack in the cabled
wooldings grows, and like rent silk
the threadbare, tear-pocked mainsail
leeches a guttering sunlight through.

Alcaeus

OCEAN BIRD

What bird is it that's traveled here, winter-fed,
from the banks of the river that rounds the earth?
A widgeon with a tawny, buff-crowned head,
and wings to compass a grown man's girth?

Alcaeus

RIVER HEBRUS

Most beautiful of rivers, its icy, stream-fed freshets
    start up in the anticlines of Rhodope
and beyond that rocky, headlong fall spill out
    into the shallows and holms, the weedy
margins of the wetlands, old groves and haycocks
    and rocked-off plots of Thracian land.

Along its way, who can say how many young girls
    will enter its waters to wash their hair,
to cool their thighs, or—as if its silvery wetness
    somehow held the chrism of their womanhood—
to raise up in their tight-cupped hands
    deep draughts of its breathtaking liquors.

Alcaeus

BEST OF ALL

Best of all is never to be born, never to see the blood-
    orange sun swelter the hills and high meadows.
But once you're born then best of all to hurry on through
    the gates of hell and, once inside, lie
down under a caprocked gash of moldering earth.

Theognis

THE COMMON EVIL

Think hard about what you angle for.
Athens won't perish by decree of Zeus
or by will of the deathless gods.
It will fall, instead, by the excesses of
her citizens who, in pursuit of money
lares and penates career headlong
toward ruin. And so there seeps into
every house a common evil, and no
bolted, latched, or twice-barred door
can keep it out, for it vaults the high
hedge and finds everyone home,
even those hiding beneath their beds.

Solon

THE BODY POLITIC

A cloud holds the power of sleet and snow,
the lightning flash of rolling thunder,
armed men the destruction of our cities,
and the poor in their ignorance are fettered
like slaves by the whims of despots and kings.

Solon

ON THE DISPENSATION OF RICHES

Not even the most lavish gallery of gold
and silver flagons, no earth-walled hoard
of gems and gilt-enameled bowls, no far-flung
fields of wheatland, no purchase of mules
and dairy cows can exceed the wealth
of a single man whose belly's full,
whose feet are warm, and who, though
poor, still enters into love with a woman
in the bee-happy season of his youth.

Solon

THE DEATH OF GERYON

With a fatally windswept shiver, the high-
lobbed arrow split the distance between his eyes,
punched up to its trim feathers, then lodged itself
bile-tipped and keening in the brainpan.

Then, like a far-gone poppy that in summer
bends to let its petals fall, he bowed his head
so the dark blood ran, fouling crest and coverts,
the black blazon of his trailing wings.

Stesichorus

AN END TO WAR SONGS

Let's set aside man-killing thoughts for the day,
forget about war altogether, and summon up a wedding
of the gods, of boards high-piled for feasting men.

Let's tune our instruments to a roundelay
to celebrate spring, for the rowan trees are coming into leaf,
and fledgling swallows are dipping in the wind.

Stesichorus

VIGIL

Custom has it it's only in spring the quince-
trees of Cydonia bloom, watered by a stream
whose wellhead spills from the fata morgana
of secret gardens and inviolate maids,

    and vine-borne flowers
  still tremble and snake beneath
    their mantling sprays.

But experience tells me that love has no one season,
that like the thunderclap of a Thracian gale
which bellows in sheeted with lightning,
it strikes year-round, blacking out the sun,

    and in the human
  heart there's nowhere to shelter
    from its violence.

Ibycus

THE WINGED SPIRIT'S AFTERTHOUGHT

I saw them there this morning
in the new-leafed crown of a hornbeam tree,
   pied wild ducks, two shag-purples
with black-chevroned throats, and one of those wide-
   winged halcyons that sailors
looking homeward call the fisher king. O,
   if only my heart could keep
the high mystery of their airborne race.

Ibycus

ARTEMON AND THE FATES

It wasn't all that long ago he skulked about
in filthy, lice-infested rags, wore wooden earrings
and around his ribs the oxhide stripped
from a cast-off shield. Sweet talker that he was,
he cadged his meals off bakery girls and local whores,
though sometimes you might find him bound
neck down on a whipping block, or strapped
to a wheel and ratcheted up as thumb-size
gobbets of his scalp tore off. How is it, then,
that this same man now rides through town
in a gilded, silk-screened litter, wears jeweled
earrings like a mix-with-all, and shades himself
with a dowager's ivory parasol?

Anacreon

JEALOUSY

Once roused,
the body's strapping blacksmith plunged me whole
into the reddened heart of bellowed coals,
struck me twice with an iron hammer,
    then doused
me in a bucket of water. So forged,
I took up arms against your faithless hair,
which I raised in my fist like the Gold-
    en Fleece.

Anacreon

THE IMAGE OF GOD

1

It was man who made god, who endowed god
with the body of a man, the voice of a man,
who dressed him in the earthy garments of a man.

2

If a workhorse or lion or unyoked ox
had eyes to paint, had hands to sculpt,
had voice to sing its tribal song,

the horse would paint god as a horse,
the lion would sculpt a lion god,
the ox would sing a divinity of oxen.

3

The Ethiopians say, "Our gods have flat noses
and black skin." The Thracians say, "The hair
of our gods is red, their eyes the color of jade."

Xenophanes

PYTHAGORAS

As folklore has it, he was walking past
   a square where the local drunk
was beating some mangy dog with a stick.
   Pitying the dog, Pythagoras
yelled, "Stop beating that poor dog. Its soul
   is that of my dead friend,
for I can hear his voice in its whimpers."

Xenophanes

PRELUDE TO A CONVERSATION

Such things should be asked before a banked-up fire
in winter, in the quiet hour after plates are cleared
and the body reclines on an overstuffed couch,
sipping wine and nibbling a bowl of chickpeas.
Such things as: "Who are you? Where do you live?
How old are you now? How old were you then,
when the blood-bent warlord laid waste your land?"

Xenophanes

AGAINST TRUTH

1

As for the lives of the gods, as for whatever
I say about anything, no one has ever been sure,
and no one ever will be. And if, by chance,
someone comes along and utters the truth,
how would we verify the truth he spoke?
For all we know with certainty is: there is
nothing we know beyond the world of seems.

2

The deathless gods never granted us
the knowledge of all things, but in time
we have pursued that knowledge,
and in time we've invented better.

3

Let this be held as resembling the truth.

Xenophanes

ON NATURE

1

Whatever becomes and grows
is all and only earth and water.

2

One end of the earth we see at our feet
where it rises to meet the air,
the other falls away unending.

3

And the sun passes over and warms the earth.

4

The sea is the source of all weather,
for without the endless coursing of the sea
there would be no wind in the trees,
no freshets spilling into rivers,
no rainwater falling from the sky.

5

Even the shield of Agamemnon,
even the goddess we call Iris,
even they are mere rainbows,
mere clouds of water and air,
of yellows, indigos, violets, blues.

6
If there is a divinity, it is
all eye, all mind, all ear.

7
It abides in one place and never moves,
nor does it bend one way or another.

8
For all that is arises from the earth,
and all that is returns to the earth.

Xenophanes

ON BEAUTY

As the ancient stories tell us, invisible
to mortal men, beauty dwells among
the high-capped rocks near a wind gap
arduous to climb. And you must almost
wear your heart out in the struggle
required to attain its height.

Simonides

ON POETRY

Like the bee, she consorts with flowers
    to concoct her dream
of a scented, pollen-yellow honey.

Simonides

ON POETRY AND PAINTING

The word is the image of the thing.

Poetry is painting that speaks.
Painting is poetry that's silent.

Simonides

THE IMAGE OF THE THING

The high-hung scarlet mainsails
    dyed with the petals
of a flowering holm oak.

•

The wind came stippling the sea
    and raising the dust
beside a chariot's wheel.

•

The water-roofed sea encloses
    our dreams in the din
of its bone-lapping combers.

Simonides

ORPHEUS

As the tidal flats resounded
  with the pathos of his song,
    unnumbering broad-winged
    shorebirds circled overhead,
and fishes leapt straight from the sea.

Simonides

HALCYON DAYS

As when, approaching winter solstice, god beds
the winds for fourteen days, storms subside
into idle weather, and we call those lollings sacred,
so, too, these days when the legendary seabird breeds.

Simonides

DANAË AND PERSEUS ADRIFT

As storm winds foundered their bolted chest
and mouthing breakers hollered them about,
she wrapped her arms around her son and wept
into his ear, "Pale child, while night fears rise
to fuel this storm, death-bound in our brass-
ribbed boat you sleep the sleep of infancy.
No salt wrack from the breakneck waves
or rumple of wind off the panels has marked
your brow in its swathe. So sleep, my child,
as I pray the sea will also sleep, my fears
will sleep, the gods will sleep and dream us
safely back to land. And if what I ask offends
the gods or breaches the mortal contract,
then I pray to be forgiven for that as well."

Simonides

THE DANCER

Like a great-horned deer run down by bloodhounds
on the Dotian plain, her wild unbroken body bends
and twists, and her head thrown back in a black
convulsion torques first this way, then that, then another.

Simonides

GIRL SINGING I

No ghosted breeze arose to shuffle
the scattered leaves, for even such small

commotions would have silenced the one
whose song fomented the hearts of men.

Simonides

GIRL SINGING II

As if the timbre of her voice
had reddened the wound
of her lipsticked mouth.

Simonides

DRAGONFLY

Being no more than a man, don't pretend
   you can tell what the new day
brings, nor that, seeing someone happy,

you know just how that happiness will end.
   Things change—we never know why—
with the zigzag speed of a long-winged fly.

Simonides

THE TRAGEDY OF LEAVES

Of all things Homer said, one thing exceeds all others:
"The tragedy of man is the tragedy of leaves."
Yet few who've heard it have taken it to heart.
For in youth we come to believe some things
will never die, that sickness, decrepitude
and age are mere phantasms of an alien mind.
Poor fools, how oversoon death will seem to them,
how like a dream, that momentary judder of existence.

Simonides

THE SPHINX'S RIDDLE ON MAN

There moves upon the earth a two-footed,
　　four-footed, three-footed creature.

It has one name, yet of all the creatures
　　who creep along on solid ground,

or test the vaulted reach of sky, or sound
　　the fathomless depths of sea,

of every creature that lives and dies, this beast
　　alone can alter its nature.

And this: its strong legs are never weaker
　　than when it travels on all four feet.

Anonymous

THE OTHER WORLD

Poor creatures of a passing day. What is a man?
What is he not? We are a scumbling shadow's
dream. And yet, there are brief moments
when the sun transfusing a cloudlet in the after-rain
reminds us of a radiance that, pitched
beyond the reach of our dark world, still touches us,
from time to time, with an unimagined glow.

Pindar

SPIRITS OF THE AFTERWORLD

On them alone raw sunlight shines
beyond the darkness that forms our element here.
    The arable plains around them
are tufted with spreading incense trees, or brailled

    with tussocky, water-colored
pools of wildflowers coming into bloom.
    And as we hear, some of them ride
on horseback through the defile of a snow-

    fed falls, others wrestle or test
themselves in footraces down a gravel bar,
        still others gather over table games
or work out verses practiced on a lyre.

    And all day long a storied
gladness fills to overbrim their hearts,
        and a fragrance spooled
from ribboned braids of frankincense

    consecrates their altar fires.
Still, on the far shore of that great divide,
        a black and sluggish river
disgorges an endless, melancholy silt.

                                        Pindar

THE CONTEST OF TWO MOUNTAINS

Just imagine this story the old wives tell.
How two sacred mountains in Boeotia
resolved to sing in contest for a laurel wreath.
The second singer ended thus: "The Cretan
guardians hid away an infant god
in the deepest reaches of a cliff-side cave,
safe from his maundering father's wrath."
So sung, the gods placed secret ballot stones
in a golden urn, and the greater share,
as it turned out, was cast in favor of the second.
But then, in a rush of unchecked anger,
the defeated mountain wrenched a boulder
from its slopes and, in an avalanche of groans,
hurled it down upon the villagers below.

Corinna

ADONIS IN THE UNDERWORLD

Of all the pleasures in the upper world,
    what I miss most is sunlight,
after that the stars, a full moon, summer's
    late season harvest of fruits,
cucumber, apple, pomegranate, pear.

Praxilla

ASTER I

Star gazer, my star, if only I were the sky,
I would watch you with ten thousand eyes.

Plato

ASTER II

Alive, you shone among us like the morning star;
now, like the evening star, your mantle lights the dead.

Plato

SOCRATES TO HIS LOVER

As we leaned to kiss, my landlocked spirit sprouted wings
and hovered there in the fan feather of his breathing.

Poor airborne, half-celestial thing, it almost seemed
she'd wanted to abandon me and fly away with him.

Plato

HAND-CARVED STONE

This seed-shaped, chalcedonic stone, the inset
for a rich man's ring, is carved with the seal
of seven cows, cows so plainly glutted
on sweet meadow grass, you almost feel

they'll wander off now they've had their fill.
And indeed they would, had the engraver
not taken it upon himself to corral
them within a double band of golden wire.

Plato

PAN

Come, love, come join me beneath this high-

branched pine, come listen to the thwarted wind
sluicing like a river through its limbs,

come sit beside these glittering, sun-thronged
pebbles and I promise you, before too long,

panpipes will animate your poppied eyes.

Plato

FOUR RIDDLES, TWO ENIGMAS

1

I am the black child of a white father,
a wingless bird whose flight outsoars
heaven's gate. If you dare look closer,

I'll dilate your eyes with mourners' tears,
for already, even as I was born,
I was thinning out into empty air.

2

One wind, two ships, ten stout men at their oars,
one captain to pilot both vessels clear.

3

I'm a brain without a head, a green brain
rising on a long-necked, luteous stem.
I'm a ball unbalanced on a flute end.
If you feel along my flanks you'll find
my mother's father secreted within.

4

No one sees me when he sees, but sees me
when he can't. He who is silent will speak,
and he who runs is never the runner.
I am wholly untrue, though what I say
is always a wholly unerring truth.

5

Say nothing and you will say my name.
But must you say something? Here again,
we encounter a small conundrum,
for in saying something you'll say my name.

6

Two sisters born from the same parents.
One sister gives birth to the other,
and once that delivery's over,
the newborn becomes the one who bears.
And so, sisters of one blood, they are
both sisters and mothers in common.

                                    Anonymous

II

HELLENISTIC
PERIOD

(c. 323–31 B.C.)

INVITATION TO OBLIVION

Why was I born? Where did I come from?
How do I happen to be where I am?
Knowing nothing, how can I learn anything?

I was nothing, and yet I was born,
and before too long I'll be nothing again,
nothing at all, of no value whatever.

And such is the lot of everyone. I say,
therefore, brim the mixing bowls with wine,
for only in oblivion is oblivion braved.

Anonymous

BETRAYAL

The nights are endless,
it's winter weather,
and the new moon sets
when the Pleiades are
halfway up the sky.

So how have I come,
wet and whimpering
as a beaten dog,
to keep trying her
double-bolted door?

Asclepiades

THE THIRD EPISTLE

Love, you've withheld yourself for too long now.
And to what end? You'll find out soon enough
there are no lovers in the underworld, no love
anywhere beyond this rounding green-housed globe
on which the future world is bred. Can you imagine
another reason why the deathless gods would envy us?
Beyond this, only dust and ashes will share our beds.

Asclepiades

TO A BED LAMP

Three times she lay in the scumbling
half-light of your glow, three times her pen
gave me her word then took it back again.

So now the hour rounds to ask: On those raw
and moonless nights ahead, when new men
come to honey in her downy, high-roofed bed,

would you grant me this one small favor?
Would you spit black smoke and gutter out?
Would you refuse them tender light to love?

Asclepiades

LOVE'S THIRD BURDEN

It was well past midnight, a winter squall,
and as if to take on love's third burden,
I'd grown sick and self-pitying from wine.
The north wind muffled my womanish sobs,
my repeated exclamations of your name,
and all down the darkened street that night
I refused all thoughts of shelter, refused
even the dim-lit warmth of a familiar door.

Instead, cold and dripping like the drowned,
I dispraised the raw spirit of the weather god:
"Is your hardened heart untouched by me?
Is there no fellow feeling I kindle in you?
Did you learn nothing when you were the one
undone by love and driven by its storm?"

Asclepiades

EROS: AN ATTESTATION

Hail wrack and thunder, cataracts of rain, shake out
    your overlapped blackness, cleave the sea
in one fell crack, level the hills in the heart-
    beat of your squadroned clouds, for if you wreck me

then I'll be wrecked. But if I survive, if I endure
    the full brunt of your iron abuse,
then I'll still go, still drag myself to her front door,
    for I'm mastered by the god who mastered Zeus,

who goaded him onward, glamoured in gold, to shower
    the cell of a doomed king's daughter.

Asclepiades

THE WAISTBAND OF HERMIONE

Chance one day found us alone together,
and, as happens, with one thing leading to another,

I found my fingers undoing the knot
that fastened the ceinture around her waist. It was shot

through with lime green, jet, and organdy threads,
and in tiny white lettering on the underside

these words were stitched: "Enjoy me as you wish,
though at your peril, for other men have handled this."

Asclepiades

PRECOCIOUS ONE

How could a girl have learned so well the ways
of men, the sidelong glance, the all-too-dewy

smile with which, having caught your lurid stare,
she releases it over her shoulder,

the way her linen robe's cinched up so high
the sunlight gilds her lotioned thighs?

Asclepiades

SHELTER

It's a good thing in the dog days for a thirsty man
to suck a thawing chunk of snow, for fishermen

after a sail-shredding winter storm to feel
the first warm gusts of spring, but better still

is when two lovers, stranded on a sandbar
by the rising tide, take one coat as their shelter.

Asclepiades

EVENING MEAL

Hurry to market, Demetrius, and purchase
    from Amyntas three salted herring,
ten nicely trimmed fillets of sole, and have him shell
    a large handful of his freshest prawns.

After that, rush over to Thauborius' stall,
    pick up one of those incense-scented
barberry wreaths he loops around with bands of silk.
    I'll be pouring out the wine by then

and lighting lamps and candles, so hurry back home
    as fast as you can. And, since you'll pass
his doorway anyhow, why don't you stop and ask
    Tryphera to come and join us, too?

Asclepiades

RELICS FOR APHRODITE'S TEMPLE

Having passed her fiftieth birthday,
the amorous, heaven-hearted Nicias
hung from hooks on the temple walls
her high-tied sandals, a braided length
of graying hair, the handheld mirror
in which she'd marked the shadowings
of age, and a basketful of feathery things
about which men are forbidden to speak.
And there they remain, a lived-through,
yellowing memorial for those who'd muse
on all the sad etcetera of human love.

Philetas

THE BOW

I once was the better of two finely recurved
    ibex horns, transversely ridged, and sanded down
to shape a hook for mounting bay-leafed garlands.
    But the horn worker soon adapted me
to even stranger sport, for while torquing me over
    the arch of his foot, he cinched both nubs
with the sturdy sinew of a crumple-horned ox.

Simmias

SPINTHER THE COOK

When Spinther the cook became a freed slave
and dared to imagine the future he'd have,

he consigned to Hermes the tools of his trade:
a pipkin, flesh hook, the well-honed blades

of a boning knife, cleaver and hatchet,
a bronze cauldron with an iron ratchet

to raise it up above the fire, a ladle,
a mortar, two club-shaped, hand-size pestles,

a sopping sponge to clean the spit,
and a wooden trough for the butchered meat.

Ariston

THE GODS

Some local kids muzzled a he-goat today,

cinched the muzzle with a purple rein,
then, yanking at its beard, quickly trained

it how to race, goaded on by horsy sounds,
around and around the temple grounds,

where a god sat gazing on their childish play.

Anyte

BEACHED DOLPHIN

No longer headlong off the black seabed
do I plunge thundering through the light-
breached air, no longer do I torque and dive
snorting past my image, my figurehead,

decked out on the prow of a windswept ship.
Still-birthed out of my substance, I lie land-
locked on a wide isthmus of bellied sand
like a promise my own death can't quite keep.

Anyte

ON A CATALANA COCK

How strange to find I miss the mad racket
of its squawk and clattering wing beats

waking me early in the blue dawn light.
A fennec fox entered its coop last night

and severed its head below the cape
with a swipe of its swift, aciculate claws.

Anyte

THE DWELLING PLACE OF CYPRIS

This high prospect is the Cyprian's, for it pleases her ever
    to look out over the sun-glazed sea and muster
    sailors to scull their beaked ships leeward.
And all around, the lumbering breakers tremble with fear.

Anyte

A STATUE OF HERMES

Here I stand, at the crossroads of three
byways, in a windswept belt of willow trees

that hedges a shingled strand behind; here,
as well, the weary traveler shelters,

and through my rocked-in wellhead purls
a fountain of unstained, spring-fed water.

Anyte

THE DROWNING

The dumb image reflected off water in a wellhead
    beguiled the three-year-old.
Fearing the worst, as mothers will, his mother struggled

    to haul him out, feet first
and dripping from his well-birth. But the boy did not
    profane with death that moss-

lit dwelling of the water nymphs. Instead, he fell
    asleep on the warming hill
of his mother's knees, and there he slumbers soundly still.

Poseidippus

EPITAPH ON A BRIDE'S TOMB

I am the tomb of the white bride Baucis,
and those who pass through my shadow
should pause to remind the underworld god
such envies are unworthy of a king.
The chiseled letters you see on this stone
are the telltale sign of his tampering—
how the bride's own father lighted her pyre
with the pine torch he had earlier struck
to illuminate the singing of the hymeneals.
But who could believe the marriage god
conspired to turn their celebrant song
into the ash tones of a funeral dirge?

Erinna

WINTER PASTORAL

At dusk, by ones and twos, the cows lug homeward
through deeply drifted banks of snow; and there,
beneath an oak tree blasted by lightning, the cowherd
dreams a dream whose meaning he'll not be spared.

Diotimus

THE TOMB OF ORPHEUS

A caprock on the skirts of Mount Olympus
marks the spot where poetry was laid to rest.

The man whose song moved Thracian swordsmen
to surrender arms, who charmed alike wild beast and stone,

who summoned from the fresh-leafed hills whole herds
of forest creatures, great flocks of broad-winged birds.

The man whom legend reminds us once intoned a chord
so deep in the heart of the underworld

the damned fell silent and the Furies wept.

Damagetus

HOMER

Just as the sun, wheeling about on axles of fire,
darkens the moon, the sacred figures in the thronging stars,
so, too, did Homer, raising up above his art

the brightest of the Muses' lamps, make shadow
of whatever accolades, whatever burnished kudos,
are heaped a hundredfold on our singers now.

Leonidas of Tarentum

THE TOMB OF THERIS

Here lies a man who made his living off well-
marked traps, who rode the breakers like a gull—

marauder of fishes, hauler of seines, prober
in the crannies of rock and cliff—who never

once sailed the crowded lanes in an open-
rigged, long-beaked quinquereme, who scorned

the gods by dying not in the bloodbath
of a battle, nor shipwrecked in the aftermath

of a hurricane, nor in any way fishermen
normally end. He died, instead, of his own

accord, dimming out like the evening light
on a cot in his wood-plank hut. No wife,

no children arranged for his burial,
but the members of the local fishermen's guild.

Leonidas of Tarentum

CICADA

Not only do I sing and sing for free
    while perched sure-footed
in the top-most branches of a poplar tree,

not only do I make my high-strung music
    for the lone uncaring
passerby and take my meal at the banquet

table of a drop of dew, but much as the Muses
    love me for those gifts
made in their name, you'll no doubt be amused

to learn it thrills me more that I've been cut
    and inlaid on Athena's
spear, an encomium to her goddess flute.

Leonidas of Tarentum

MICE

If it weren't for the fact that you gnaw and scratch
at the latch of my hollow meal bin, I'd think
(for there's pretty thin pickings within this shack)
you skittery creatures must feed on dark.

An old man is content with two barley cakes
and some sea salt, the sum my father figured
was our lot in life. So why keep me awake
all night then leave me to sweep your turds?

You'll never find a smidgen on my bare floor.
Wouldn't a rich man offer you better fare?

Leonidas of Tarentum

SOCHARES THE CYNIC

A wallet, an untanned rag of goat hide,

a flask too thick with crud to clean, a gnawed-
on hardwood walking stick, and a straw-

colored purse without a copper in it.
With these scrubby relics famine decked out

the alleyway where Sochares died.

Leonidas of Tarentum

TELESO THE SHEPHERD

Between the limbs of an ancient plane tree,

in a last offering to the well-hung,
goat-legged, goat-fucker Pan, Teleso strung

a scrap of hide and the whittle-point staff
he'd kept on hand for the hungering wolf

that dared to test the stones of his fold.
He hung his cheese pails there as well, and blood-

wet dog collars for the daylight to bleach.

Leonidas of Tarentum

HOMAGE TO CLITO

Here stands Clito's wattle hut, here the half-
acre of harrowed, well-composted tilth

he harvested year-round, and near that stands
a trellised vineyard, a patch of brushwood,

the hollowed cork and osier-woven hives—
for eighty years all he needed to live.

Leonidas of Tarentum

EUALCES THE CRETAN

The great beast that for a fortnight wrought
   such slaughter on sheep and cattle alike,
that showed no fear of snarling dogs
   or torches staked out against it,
that very same beast this half-wit slew
   with a single blow from his mattock.
The next morning, he skinned the hide and strung
   it up in a bitternut tree.

Leonidas of Tarentum

TRAVELERS' AID

For you who've hiked here from the bridle path,

don't pause to sip from this thickening rill
of muddy water, but continue uphill

past the next high ridge where the heifers graze
on blue-green riverines of mountain grass.

And as you approach the cowherd's tent,
you'll find welling up through fissured stone

clear waters snow-fed from summits in the north.

Leonidas of Tarentum

AT THE GRAVE OF CHARIDAS

Is it Charidas who rests beneath this stone?
If it's the son of Arimmas you mean, it is.

And what sort of world surrounds you there?
A great darkness is all, a darkness beyond imagining.

Is it true what they say, the insensible dead
will be born again? *All lies, lies and superstition.*

Then what of Pluto? People say that he returned.
Pluto is a myth and nothing more. We die forever,

we remain that way, it's a fate that has no end.
If it's true what you say, wouldn't that undo

whatever small hope the living require to drag
ourselves from day to day? *What I say is true.*

If it's comforting words you're after, if it's
pipe dreams you'd be guided by, then turn deaf ears

on the voice that speaks beneath this stone
and address your questions to the living.

Callimachus

AT THE TEMPLE OF APHRODITE

Come stand with me on this shelving bench
of beach rock, and while the bone-lapping

sea waves thresh the shore, observe
the sanctum of her olive grove.

How its augured, allegoric shade embowers
the sacrament of a wellspring where,

dipping its bill, a yellow kingfisher
sips from a rill of running water.

Mnasalcas

THE BIDDING OF THE HARBOR GOD

Take your thwarts, oarsmen, it's time to carve
new sea-lanes through the breasting swells.
Wild gales no longer avalanche the shoals
or harrow the rigging of a sailor's nerve,

and already out of mud and clay swallows
build their jug-nests underneath your eaves.
So quickly now, before the gulled moon leaves
its slumberous lightweight in the meadows,

break loose your trim ship's hawsers, haul
the anchor from its harbor nest, and stand
up into the trade winds off the headland
your woven, patched, and thrice-stitched sails.

Antipater of Sidon

PRAISE SONG

Winter's whey-colored shadows have leeched out
from the hills, and the fields are purpling with violets.

Hedgerows garland the black farmland, willow brakes
form a shaded warren for small spring hares

and dew-logged meadows for the opening rose.
The shepherd plays his panpipes on a scrubby knoll,

the goatherd gloats over his white kids, and bellied
sails already blossom on the sea-lanes, already

the wine drinkers braid their hair with berried vines.
From the rotting carcass of an oxen, a beeline

streams to the honey-heavy combs, and the race of birds
rehearses: shearwaters slanting off breakers,

swallows arrowing the dripping eaves, plovers
calling from the mudflats, vireos from the groves.

And if new leaves brighten the sallow and barberry,
if the shepherd pipes while his snubbed flocks graze

and bluefish circulate the waterways, who's to say
an old man can't raise a raspy, heartfelt voice in praise.

Meleager

LOVE SONG FOR ZENOPHILA

Already the hillside violets are spilling
into bloom, and the wax-red, star-shaped lilies,

and the lolling narcissi that seek their reflection
in the morning rain. But the rose of persuasion,

the heart's own darling, makes other flowers
seem less lovely than they are. Why do meadows

even bother to host such excess every spring?
You alone are the image of such flowerings.

Meleager

TO A CICADA IN THE PLANE TREE ABOVE ME

Day-worker drunk on dew, your field song fills
the surrounding hills, and, squat on the rug
of an alder leaf—your scrubbing rigged
to amplify your carapace—you sound a trill
whose note denatures to a human cry.
Would that you would sing, instead, a descant
summoning daylong sleep, or strike some strain
to ease me from love and sorrow again.

Meleager

TO A MOSQUITO

Be my conscript messenger, take light-winged
flight to the porch of Zenophila's ear, and there
lay out the argument I would move her by:

"Nightlong he waits for your knock on his door,
while you, who all too quickly forget your former
lovers, lie rolled in a plush untroubled sleep."

Go now, little airborne courier, and be careful
you don't rouse whoever's drowsing at her side,
for I wouldn't wound even a rival's heart

with those same feelings that ravage mine.
Do your job well, bring her back to me this once,
and I'll settle you with a hero's prize.

The curried pelt of a lioness will hood your head,
and your hands will wield a bludgeon spiked
with jagged scraps of iron and bronze.

Meleager

FIRE

It was midafternoon when I saw Alexis
loitering in the marketplace, the late-
season harvest of fruits and vegetables
heaped in panniers and wooden tubs.

And while the world seemed all of overfill,
standing out in that shadeless square
I got burned twice, once by the sun
and once by the way he glanced at me.

Even so, the dark was little comfort
when it finally came, for though the sun
was safely laid to rest, my dreams
refreshed the lifelong memory of that scald

across my cheek, the elemental mark
that burns from appetite and carnal fire.

Meleager

EARTHENWARE JAR

I'd prefer to take my wine tonight
in an unglazed earthenware jar.
That way, each time it meets my lips,
I'll taste and be reminded of
the clay from which I came,
the clay in which I'll one day dwell
and one day I'll turn into.

Zonas

III

ROMAN

PERIOD

(c. 31 B.C.–A.D. 500)

ON THE BIRTH OF CHRIST

To find heaven in a cattle stall.
No, to find something stranger still.

To find heaven's vault has been unroofed
by an infant in a feeding trough.

Anonymous

WILDROSE SEASON

It's the season of wildrose and mint, Sosylos,
the season of chickpeas and first-cut sprouts,
of smelts and salted cheeses, of curly-edged
lettuce whose new leaves light transfuses
with a half-remembered glow. Even so,
have you noticed how this year something's changed?
How we no longer take our morning walks
along the newly poppied shore, picnic
under the plane trees, or hurry over drinks
the sinking lozenge of the evening sun?
How Antigenes and Bacchios, our sun-bronzed,
buff, athletic friends, were flirting yesterday,
and today we carry them to their graves?

Philodemus the Epicurean

O

O feet, O legs, O thighs before which I've knelt down,
O honeyed cunt, O belly glazed with sweat and cum,
O rowing, unwinged shoulder blades, O breasts
and blushing neck inclined, O eyes I've waded into
just to plumb their depthless almond calms,
O bracing arms, O body that in loving bends and tenses
like an orchard limb, O fruited kiss, O breathless outbursts
that in loving raise a goose's flesh along my arms.
Summoned from such raptures to engage your stares,
I ask you, fellow countrymen, why should I care
if Italian blood runs in her veins, her manner's
by your standards odd, or her voice has never lifted
to the clarities of Sappho's songs? Don't stars
still burn for the hell-bent Argive hero who hoisted up
Medusa's head, who slew an oceanic beast
to marry the fair daughter of an Ethiope king?

Philodemus the Epicurean

WATER DRINKERS

I don't dread the Pleiades setting
when I'm out at sea, nor sea storms
pummeling the back-braced keel, nor
lightning striking off a bowsprit

nearly so much as I've come to dread
the man who sits and sips his water
so that he can better remind us later
exactly what each and everyone said.

Antipater of Thessalonica

STAR-CROSSED BRIDE

It wouldn't be the marriage god whose hand
her hand would take that night, but a god
out of the underworld who'd come to stand
at the foot of her high-strung bridal bed.

As new brides will, delaying her rousing
husband's hungers, she'd fled on foot
to a childhood haunt near the summerhouse.
But the unleashed guard dogs caught her scent

and, lathering after her, ran her down.
And we, who'd hoped all night to see her rapt
in the full blush of a newlywed, found,
instead, mattered bits of gnawed-on scraps

(scarcely enough to even bury well)
scattered amongst the garbage from the festival.

Antiphanes

CORPSE

Tell me, how can we possibly call this mess
a man's remains, broken up like an urn
as the blunt waves hurled him time and again
against the seawall's jagged rock? Here lies
his hairless head with all the teeth knocked out,
and there, five fingers of a chewed-off hand,
the birdcage of his unfleshed ribs, a foot
without strappings, and a leg that's so disjointed
you could fold it like an easel into threes.
Are we to believe these random bits composed
one thing? That we called that thing a man?
Blessed are those, I tell you, who were never born
to see sun rise from its bloodshot grave.

Philip

PISO THE FISHERMAN

Bowed down by forty years at sea,
his hands leathered from hauling seines,
he left to Hermes two wicker creels,
his rods fitted out with tested line,

the oars that over decades dipped
like dolphins past the gunwales,
hooks he'd fretted from the throats and lips
of countless deep-sea catch, the guild-

stitched nets, the floats he'd used to mark
his traps, a barbed trident, a scarred
slab of quarried flint still flush with spark
enough to strike five hundred fires,

and, twice-tarred, a lagging anchor,
the lug that holds fast ships offshore.

Philip

CLYTOSTHENES THE MUSICIAN

The man whose now-enfeebled feet
once danced as if on embers, leaves

to the goddess of the lion car his wine-
stained, sweat-stained tambourine,

his raucous, hollow-rimmed cymbals,
a double flute on which the squall

of his night song rehearsed
its riot in the marketplace,

and the knife with which, in vain,
he once tried to open up a vein.

Philip

HOMER

Heaven will sooner banish Orion
and let sunlight kindle the midnight sky,
the sea will sooner provide well water
to ships dismasted far from shore,
the numberless dead will sooner come back
to walk green earth amongst the living,
than oblivion will take these pages
and snuff out the memory of Homer.

Philip

THE HALLOWING

I don't know whether to honor it as a battle shield,
the faithful ally with whom I countered squad
on squad in slaughter on that blazoned field,

or as my well-caulked seacraft since, for the sunless hours
it took for me to escape the doomed ship back to shore,
it buoyed up my bloodied head. But this is clear:

only under its aegis did I make it home.

Julius Diocles

HECTOR

And a passing stranger asked of the rough-hewn
slab of stone, "Who fathered the man beneath you?

What was his name? The country he called home?
What brought him to lie in such desolate ground?"

"He is the son of Priam," the stone slab answered.
"His home was built of lumber from the alder

groves of Ilion. Hand to hand in blood-gored
mail he died defending his land. Remember!

For on the brazen tablets of the future
time will etch the man-killing name of Hector."

Archias

THE BATTLE OF THERMOPYLAE

The very same battalions that recharted
the course of earth and sea, that sailed dry land
and marched in heavy armor over water,

it took, by count, three hundred bronze-beaked
Spartan spears to turn back in a rout.
Great shame now attends the hills and sea.

Parmenion

THE RIVAL OF HESIOD

Yesterday, while leafing through the pages
of *Works and Days*, I happened to look up
and see you coming through the olive grove.
Without thinking twice, I tossed the book aside
and asked, "Why should I waste my time
on work by old gray beards like him,
or with any day other than today?"

Marcus Argentarius

THE FATES

When snow clouds blanketed the saddleback peaks,
a grazing herd of great-horned deer traversed
the vale to warm themselves in the scrubby steam
that issued from a spring in the meadow.
But fortune had plotted to hobble the deer
and lock them hock high in the crusting ice.
So it was only a matter of time before the party
of local fishermen who, with creels and fishnets
empty, had stumbled home earlier in the day
would ply their mallets and filleting knives
to scrag the herd, roast the innards in a high-built fire,
and, one by one, offer up blessings to familiar gods.

Apollonides

THE OCTOPUS

Having found it enisled in a rock pool after
the tide withdrew, the fisherman snatched
an octopus up and, afraid that it might latch
itself around his wrist, pitched it over

onto a grassy clearing in the underbrush.
With a woozily unhinged liquid swirl,
it oozed over sideways and as if by will
slumped against a rabbit asleep in the grass.

Like melted wax, the tentacles spilled,
hardened, then contracted around
the bone cage of the rabbit's head.
By grace of the gods (he imagines still),

the fisherman's haul from the sea trove
was redoubled by a second haul on shore.

Bianor

THE DREAM OF PEACE

When, for the second time in as many days,
the hard-hit ruler of the underworld
received as lading shipped in wooden bays
three hundred dead mown down in war,
he said, "They are every one a Spartan.
Look, the same as it was yesterday, each
unswabbed wound's been struck in front.
Not one man turned to escape this fate."
Striding among the corded dead, he swore
an oath to them, "Unflagging warriors
of the upper air, put aside your swords,
unfasten your breastplates, hunger no more
for the killing fields your dark blood has steeped.
I shall forge your sleep as an endless peace."

Bassus

GRIEF

As she was lighting the pyre beneath one son,
she was told about her other son drowning,
shipwrecked off the coastline. A double sorrow
halved her heart, one part fire, the other water.

Honestus

OXEN

Not only are we rigged out for plowing
eyed-in furrows through the rocky ground,
but strapped as well for heavy hauling,
for dragging warships back onto land.

Twice-blessed with both the plowman's
and the oarsman's gift, we've come now
to query the sea gods. Why is it, then,
you can't yoke a dolphin to the harrow?

Leonidas of Alexandria

DAYS

Dawn after dawn slips past us unremarked.
And then, one day, while we're idly engaged
in hanging out the laundry or pruning
the garden roses back, out of nowhere
the dark one comes. The next thing we know,
we've been melted down into candle wax,
or turned on a spit over roasting coals,
or puffed out like a bladder blown into.

Ammianus

THE INVENTION OF GLASS

Having split it from a chiseled block of quarry stone,
the smithy took the flinty chip and tossed it into a fire
he'd laid and bellowed in a rock pit near his shop.

To his surprise, the chip caught fire, sputtered out,
then caught again and burned the bluer part of flame.
The heat, he thought, grew hotter then, so much so

that the stone's own nature seemed to change,
like melting wax, and overspill the flame. To the smithy
it seemed a sign from god that stone would run that way,

and he shuddered to imagine the upshot if,
like a slain man from whom dark blood runs,
the source of that guttering stream should die.

And so, with the pike end of his blackened tongs,
he dug down into the heart of fire, lifted
that radiant nugget out and held it aloft

in the smoky air, where it shone for a moment,
effulgent as a star, a star that in the heavens marks
some long-awaited miracle to come.

Mesomedes

THE EMBRACE

Last evening, as you paused in the doorway
to say good-bye, you embraced me whether
in this world or another I couldn't say.
This is all the more puzzling to discover

since I clearly recall almost everything
you did. How you nodded attentively when
I spoke, how you fiddled with your rings,
how you lavishly praised the food and wine.

But as to whether you really bent and kissed me,
my mind remains a blank. For if, in fact,
you did, if, in fact, you lowered your eyes
and pressed your lips to mine, how is it that

this morning I don't cross the market in one stride,
don't haunt the back alleys like a deathless god?

Strato

LUST

These young Turks with their oily skin and half-
cocked stares eyeing traders in the marketplace,
they're like ripe figs couched in the rock cleft
of a precipice: sweet plunder for wasps and scavenging
birds, but beyond the reach of old men like me.

Strato

DRUNKENNESS

I've drunk enough to loose those twice-tied silk
constraints on thought and tongue. The lamp's blue
flame is doubled on itself, and though I squint
and start over again, I count each guest by twos.

Not only do I quiver at the sight of the wine
waiter in his bee-like dance from guest to guest,
but wholly out of season I'm still inclined
to cast hot glances at the busboy's ass.

Strato

REPROACH

What do you think such shapeless clothes disguise,
Menippus, you who only yesterday
knotted your robes in such a way your thighs
would show? And why do you amble past me

without a word or glance in my direction?
Even as I ask these questions, I know what time
won't say. It has come, hasn't it, that thing
I warned would one day come?

Strato

THE ORACLE

Word of mouth has it that Eudoxus learned
    from a black bullock with narrow horns

the plan fate plotted for his future.
    But how? And how could he be sure

it spoke to him? So far as I can tell, nature
    never granted bulls the power

of human speech, nor calves a gift for chatter.
    Perhaps, while grazing in a pasture,

it lowed and twitched its tail up in the air,
    or met his eyes with its gormless stare,

and by such means conveyed to him: "Eudoxus,
    your last day on earth is closing fast."

For while stumbling outside that night to pee,
    he dropped dead under an alder tree.

Diogenes Laertius

ON THE RISE OF CHRISTIANITY

1

In the brutal aftermath
of the gods, is it true
that I am dead as well?
That I appear to be alive

only by pretending
my looted dream is life?
Or am I, after all, alive,
and life itself is dead?

2

Having lived in peace
for seventy years, scholiast
of the ancient texts,
it's to this dank place

that I've been sent
to finish out my days,
a lone senator of
the unnumbering dead.

3

In tears I was born,
in tears I will die,
and life in between
is the history of tears.

Like the grieving sea,
the human race weeps
incessantly, and a tear
is the lens of eternity.

Palladas

THE OLD SICKNESS

Ten thousand times I've sworn an oath
to never write another line,
nevermore labor like some smith

to catch a fall of light through pine,
for poetry's prize is nothing less
than backbiting and belittlement.

But then, tending my own business,
it happens I catch sight of her
observing herself in a looking glass

or braiding back a shock of hair,
and fight it as I may, that same
old sickness afflicts me as before.

Palladas

THE SUPPLIANT

When I finally found her alone in her room,
I got down on all fours and begged her for it,
took her scented knees in hand and from
some aching place inside I raised the goblet
of my supplication. "Won't you save the life
of an old man who, for all intents and purposes,
is almost dead? Whose numbered breaths now chafe
his lungs? An old man who, nevertheless,
is saddled with the cravings of a teenage boy?"
I think it really got to her. A hot tear clarified
her bracing stare. But as I pressed my plea,
the tear dried up and (with what I feared a gesture
of revulsion) she raised her hand to consign
my wish to the hardscrabble of some foreign land.

Rufinus

RUMOR

It's been said I no longer chase young boys,
that, having traded in my discus for a doll,
my cravings have turned to girls. It's said as well
that instead of a street arab's unscrubbed face,

his close-cropped, licey, sweat-black hair,
I choose face powders, lipsticks, rouge. Oh yes,
and dolphins feed in the woods of Erymanthus,
and a herd of green deer in the plashy air.

Rufinus

A GARLAND FROM THE ROMAN EMPIRE

River Acheron

Welling with the tears of ten thousand streams,
it carries on its back the pains of men.

Licymnius

Echo

Garrulous counterfeit of every tongue, it's her
who shadows the highland where the trill of birds
is doubled in the murmur of tongueless words.

Satyrus

Echo

Ear mime, word's wag, dregs in the wineglass of a voice.

Evodus

The Mineral Kingdom

All is ashes and sniggering and emptiness.
Whatever is, is only ever nothingness.

Glycon

IV

EARLY

BYZANTINE

PERIOD

(c. A.D. 500–600)

A HIGH HOUSE IN CONSTANTINOPLE

From the overlook of his skied estate,
we watched the old copper of a predawn
sea diluted by the tin of sunlight.
And when, at last, our vaulted windows shone,

misted over by the clear-water breath
of a feathering cloud, it was obvious
that the house no longer cared to bathe
in any other light but that till dusk.

Paulus

THE BITE

Word has it that a man who's bitten by a rabid dog
will see that dog reflected in a pool of standing water.
Which makes me ask, since I see you now in every bog
or well I pass, in every cup of upturned wine,
should I assume such ghostings are a symptom of
my sickness? Of a heart that's bitten to the bone?

Paulus

PETITION

Like the numbering dead, all night I wind
myself in sheets, and when daylight finds

my bedside with its promise of some rest,
the thronging swallows chatter, thrash, and raise

a daylong riot in the dripping eaves.
Still, no matter how hard I shut my eyes,

her face appears. So why do their black wings
heckle me? I'm not that roused, half-cocked king

who cut the tongue from Philomela's mouth.
Go mourn her lover in the sun-scorched south,

go weep on the rocks near the hoopoe's nest,
but leave me to conjure my happiness.

Leave me to my season of sleep, my dream
to be islanded in her alien arms.

Agathias

A LATRINE IN THE SUBURBS OF SMYRNA

How quickly the pricey kickshaws of the rich
and mighty get translated into a ditch

of human excrescence. All those silver fish
splayed on corallines of mullet-roe relish,

the guinea fowl larded with peacock's brain,
the pan-fried coxcombs, sweetmeats of tamarind,

whole pig's heads basted with seri-flower brooms,
pheasant eggs coddled in a butterfat cream.

In a right-about of the alchemist's trick,
their gold's new-minted in the tender of shit,

and all of that edible gurry of wealth
gets siphoned underground in rivers of filth.

Agathias

TROY

What's become of your steep-walled battlements now?
The treasure hordes banked like cordwood
in your temple halls? The mounded heads
of fatted lambs you'd roast all day
over hardwood fires? And where the wicker
caskets your wealthy women brimmed with oils?
The gilded emblems of your deathless gods?

All is lost to the bloodbath on the Scamander plain,
the corruptions of time, the spiraling of fortune's course.
Still, if it's true these reavers brought you down,
it's also true your dream of empire still survives
in the storehouse of our memory, the old gold
of armorial coin, the vulgar joke about a wooden horse
the drunken host whispers to his dinner guests.

Agathias

DEATH OF A LOCAL MUSICIAN

As the ancients tell us, when Orpheus died,
the plaintive strain of his broadcast song
continued on beyond him, resounding
over time in the throats of nightingales
near his tomb. But when you died,
I suspect, dear friend, his music stopped
for good, for in the rhythm of your mind,
in the quick, feathery, birdlike way
your aerial fingers picked their chords,
his primordial music's echo breathed.

Leontius

INVITATION TO A VOYAGE

Already the newly greening fields are freaked
with pink, bud-bursting rose. Already along
the cypress lanes cicadas lighten the bull work
of farmhands at their plows. Already the martin,
mindful parent, has housed her raggy brood
in mud-made chambers underneath the eaves.
And now the drowsing sea roads, no longer
scuttling full-rigged warships in the shallows,
bear cargo blessed by the west wind god.
Landlocked sailors, before you stow your gear,
heap up at the altar of Priapus large slabs
of cuttlefish and squid, so that when the oars-
men take their thwarts and spring tides haul us
windward, we'll all set sail with iron hearts
into the iron heart of the Ionian Sea.

Theaetetus

PAN

Wood walker, tree lover, husband of Echo,
    I dwell in the beetling rock-faced hills,
shaggy scout and keeper of broad-horned sheep.

    Goat-legged, cloven-hoofed man,
I once left home to engage head-on a closing
    breach of battle-armed Assyrians.

Let others stand on the citadels. The common
    part of me is Marathon
and the men who fought at Marathon.

Theaetetus

AMYMONE AND POSEIDON

Description of a statue in the public gymnasium, Zeuxippos

From her rosewood desk Amymone stares,
binding up lengths of her plaited hair,

her face unveiled, her upturned gaze
fixed on the naked sea king's eyes.

Beside her, oiled and long-muscled
as an otter, he clinches in the hold

of one massive fist, his token
gift: a live, still-dripping dolphin.

Christodorus

THE WRESTLER

Description of a statue in the public gymnasium, Zeuxippos

I couldn't tell you his name, that violent man

    with a trailing beard and a gaze that stilled
the hearts of all who tested him in battle.
His hair had a banded snake-like spill,

his tendons fretted at his skin's constraint,

    and when the fight was on, his skills
became the hammer and anvil of an iron will.
Down his back, a long, ropey muscle

wrapped around the cudgel of his knotted spine.

Christodorus

NOTES

ARCHAIC AND CLASSICAL PERIODS (c. 700–323 B.C.)

ARCHILOCHUS

Considered by many to be the inventor of the Greek elegy, Archilochus is doubtless one of three poets (Callinus and Tyrtaeus being the other two) to hold that distinction. Regardless, it would be hard to overestimate his importance in the history of the lyric poem, for he affected its future in at least two significant ways. He is the first poet to set aside the stock figures of literary tradition and build whole poems around his day-to-day experience of the world. He also possessed the intelligence and audacity to deploy those poems in forthright assessment of the aristocratic values that governed his world. Having claimed for poetry the domain of everyday life, and having vested that poetry with the force of social commentary, Archilochus endowed the lyric poem with a limitless capacity for self-renewal, a capacity that helped to ensure its place—and, indeed, its centrality—in the future of Western literature.

"Eclipse"
This refers to one of two solar eclipses that occurred in the poet's lifetime, most likely the one on April 6, 648 B.C. The "god of gods" refers, of course, to Zeus, king of the gods, father of the Olympians, governor of the universe.

"Portent"
By identifying himself as a warrior-poet, Archilochus broke with the traditional image of the poet-maker; that is, as someone who composed in inspired moments of leisure. At the same time, he debarred from his poems those grandly heroic figures who formed the stock in trade of Homeric poetry, opting instead for an unembellished portrait of human life. This fragment appears to anticipate a coming war.

"Prayer"
The goddess referred to is Pallas Athena, daughter of Zeus, goddess of wisdom, said to favor Odysseus among all other Greeks. In The Iliad, Homer describes her as "gray-eyed" and draped by "a hundred golden tassels, all of them tightly braided."

"Abantian Warriors"

Plutarch tells us that Abantian warriors were "the first to cut their hair in this fashion . . . because they were warlike and willing to fight hand to hand, and had learned better than any other people to bring their enemy to close quarters . . . Thus they cut their hair short so as not to give their enemies a hold on their heads."

"The Shield"

Plutarch also tells us that, while visiting Sparta, Archilochus was driven from the city for having claimed that it's better to abandon one's arms on the field than be slain, an attitude at odds with the Spartan military ethic. At odds, as well, with the Homeric heroes who fought for their armor as though it were the very material of their honor. Nevertheless, Archilochus was greatly revered on his native island of Paros, revered for both his courage in battle and his sardonic regard for the boastings of soldiers, the pretensions of generals, the false glamour of war.

TYRTAEUS

"Arete"

Tyrtaeus lived in that transitional period when Sparta changed from being just another Greek city to a community forged from a strict ethos of military discipline. Although the term "arete" denoted in Homeric times a particular kind of "goodness" assigned to those with special skills—wrestling, for example, or public speaking—Tyrtaeus played a role in delimiting its meaning to physical courage on the battlefield: "No one is a 'good man' in war if he cannot stand the sight of blood . . . or come up and reach out for the enemy." This fragment embodies the kind of call to arms Tyrtaeus was famous for. The weight that fame was accorded is noted in the *Suda Lexicon*: "The Lacedaemonians swore that they would either capture Messene or die, and when the god gave them an oracle to take a general from the Athenians, they took the poet Tyrtaeus, a man who was lame. By exhorting them to valour he captured Messene in the twentieth year." We also learn from Athenaeus that on military expeditions it was customary after the evening meal for each man to sing a poem by Tyrtaeus.

ALCMAN

Alcman of Sparta is the earliest of the Greek choral poets whose work survives in any appreciable form, and, according to at least one ancient source, he was the first poet to compose love poems and publish erotic verses. First or not, his innovative spirit led him to experiment with a variety of forms and conventions. It's worth recalling that, during the period in which he lived, Sparta imported

poets and musicians—from Lesbos, Crete, Athens, Asia Minor—and this con-
fluence of traditions, nourished in a culture that promoted arts festivals and
ceremonies, led to the rich development of both choral and literary poetry.

"At the Feast of the Bacchants"
The mysterious woman addressed here appears to be part human and part divine,
and the cheese made from lion's milk appears to be an offering to Dionysus.

"Kingfisher"
Apparently written in old age, these lines make use of an odd but appealing
scrap of bird lore. Antigonus of Carystus wrote a book of "wonders" wherein he
claims that, when the aging male halcyon (the kingfisher was believed to be
such a bird) loses its strength and can no longer fly, the female takes him on
her wings and carries him wherever she goes.

SAPPHO

It may be difficult for a modern reader to fully appreciate how unusual Sappho's
poetry was in its day, or how profoundly it marked the range and register of the
lyric poem. In Hermogenes' *Kinds of Style,* Sappho's work is admired for its abil-
ity "to describe in simple terms pleasures that are not base, the beauty of a place,
for example, the variety of plant life, the diversity of streams, and so on." But
what distinguishes her from other poets who share this respect for the natural
world is how she used that world to exalt the full range of her fervent and
uncommon passions. In *Orations,* Themistius observes: "We allow Sappho . . .
to be immoderate and excessive in praise of the beloved, for loved and lover were
both private individuals, and there was no danger in it if the loved ones should
become elevated by praise. For this love has a nobility, and noble the beloved."
So admired was Sappho's work that Plato ordained her "the tenth muse," and
Plutarch in *Virtues of Women* forswore the usual equivocations in ranking
women poets: "if we show, by comparing Sappho's poems with Anacreon's . . .
that the art of poetry . . . is not one art when practiced by men and another when
practiced by women but is the same, will anyone be able to find just cause for
blame in our demonstration?" Surely few poets in history have attracted such a
distinguished list of poet-translators: Hardy, Shelley, Dante Gabriel Rosetti,
Byron, Housman, Tennyson, and Swinburne among them.

"To Anactoria"
Despite gaps in the papyrus, it seems the beginning and middle of this poem
survived intact. One of the best known of Sappho's works, it is also the clear-
est and most compelling statement of her philosophy. Namely, that contrary to

the heroic, masculine ideal of war, action, and physical bravery, the greatest splendor is to be found in human love, and in the physical presence of the beloved, a sympathy Sappho shared with Socrates (although, as time has shown, not always with history). The poem is composed as an epistle, a letter addressed to Anactoria, a woman who appears to have gone away to Lydia with her soldier-husband.

"The Conversation"

In a celebrated passage from *On the Sublime*, Longinus cites this poem as an example of the poet's genius: "Sappho everywhere chooses the emotions that attend delirious passion from its accompaniments in actual life. Wherein does she demonstrate her supreme excellence? In the skill with which she selects and binds together the most striking and vehement circumstances of passion. . . . Are you not amazed how at one instant she summons, as though they were all alien from herself and dispersed, soul, body, ears, tongue, eyes, color? . . . The effect desired is that not one passion only should be seen in her, but a concourse of the passions."

"Evening Star"

Written in dactylic hexameters, the original fragment is believed to be part of a wedding song sung at the approach of evening to mark the end of the wedding feast. Though scholars disagree about where this fragment appeared in the song, some have suggested that it might have served as a summons for the bride and bridegroom, traditionally seated at separate ends of the feast, to come together and go forward into the next stage of the ceremony. Following that suggestion, the last line of the fragment is my interpolation.

"Six Fragments for Atthis"

It's worth remembering that for Sappho and other poets of the period the weaving and wearing of garlands was not some poetic gesture or symbolic ruse, but a very purposeful activity, the physical practice of adorning oneself (or one's lover) with braidings of violets, crocuses, anise, chervil, wild rose, myrtle, and so on. As one of Sappho's fragments explains, the gods "look favorably on what's adorned with flowers but turn away from what is ungarlanded." The various contexts in which this practice appears in her poems—and it appears often— suggest that Eros found this adornment especially appealing: "And girls ripe for wedlock weave garlands."

"The Dance"

While this is, most likely, only the beginning of a poem, one still marvels at how tonally and emotionally complete it feels. Indeed, it may well be that part of the profound influence Sappho has had on lyric poetry derives from our understanding (or, more likely, our intuition) of the poetic possibilities contained in such fragmentary utterances.

ALCAEUS

From Mytilene, the chief city of Lesbos, Alcaeus spent much of his life either in political exile or fighting the reform movement (he was a fierce defender of the aristocracy) that besieged his native island. His influence can be seen in the work of Horace, where a number of his forms and subjects were borrowed. Alcaeus also holds the distinction of being the earliest known poet to employ the metaphor "ship of state," and while he was often accused of overusing this trope, it accurately reflects his priorities. As Atheaneus observes in *Scholars at Dinner,* "Alcaeus, who was completely devoted to the Muses if ever anyone was, puts manly achievements before poetic achievements, since he was warlike to a fault."

"Battle Tackle"
The armory detailed in this poem includes only the most expensive and up-to-date weapons of the time, including the highly innovative hollow shield, introduced with hoplites in the seventh century B.C., which allowed for much swifter movement on the battlefield.

"Dog Star"
This is a lyric adaptation from Hesiod's hexameters in *Works and Days,* each detail having found its precedent in that earlier text. The ancient poets were comfortable with imitations and borrowings from other texts and little afflicted by the modern obsession with "originality."

"Storm Season"
Heraclitus points out that this poem is both a description of a storm and a political allegory anticipating conflict with the tyrant Myrsilus.

"Ocean Bird"
Ocean (*Okeanos*) was believed to be a river encircling the earth.

"River Hebrus"
Although Alcaeus' interests tended toward politics and war, he showed surprising sensitivity to the natural world. It appears that at some point he must have visited Thrace, for this poem describes its landscape with the rapt attention one associates with firsthand experience.

THEOGNIS

The poems attributed to Theognis—some six hundred elegiac couplets variously divided into three hundred to four hundred individual poems—form the only example of a complete corpus by an Archaic poet. Unfortunately, his value as a poet hardly warrants such abundance. A nobleman from Megara, Theognis was something of a self-styled authority on human behavior, and he was given to admonitions about how to lead a virtuous life. To his mind, such a life was spent preserving his own aristocratic codes and bemoaning the social and economic elevation of the lower classes, "the illiterate horde," as one poem puts it, "that knows nothing of laws or judicial practice and wears out its goatskins grazing like deer beyond the city walls." Still, even through the haze of this maddeningly prosaic imagination, occasional flashes of brilliance occur.

"Best of All"
This poem would become a classic expression of Greek pessimism, and one finds its sentiment repeated often in later poems, including a famous ode by Sophocles and Philip's poem "Corpse."

SOLON

One of the so-called Seven Sages, Solon was a remarkable and many-faceted character. As a statesman and poet, he established one of the earliest precedents for the collaboration of political and aesthetic life, a collaboration the modern age still finds it difficult to imagine. Emerging from the obscurity of preliterate Greece to become the first truly Athenian poet, he helped lay the ground for Athens' golden age and future governmental democracy. Perhaps even more unthinkable to us today, his poems served to communicate, argue, defend, and promulgate his sociopolitical policies. Easterling and Knox provide a fascinating account of one such occasion: Feigning insanity and disguised as an invalid, Solon appeared in the marketplace to recite a hundred-line poem agitating for Athenian perseverance in the seizure of the island of Salamis. And, indeed, Athens did persist, eventually conquering the island and thereby removing a growing threat to its harbors.

"The Body Politic"
Though the precise reasons are unknown to us, it appears that Solon's sagacity in both political and human affairs convinced Athenians to entrust him with the authority to rewrite their laws. Seeking to close the gap between landed gentry and dispossessed peasants, his new laws led to far-reaching social reforms, one of which was the abolition of *hectemoroi* ("sixth-parters"). A form of indentured slavery, this policy required poor farmers, in exchange for protection from neigh-

boring threats, to give one-sixth of their harvests to their guardians. Through a series of laws referred to as "the Disburdening," Solon abolished this practice, as well as one that permitted the enslavement of those who defaulted on debts. By his decree all citizens gained the right of appeal to the courts and to be tried by a jury of their peers—enactments that, as Aristotle noted in *Constitution of Athens,* "more than all else . . . strengthened the arm of the common people."

STESICHORUS

Stesichorus was a highly innovative poet, introducing narrative elements into choral poetry (his name means, literally, "arranger of the chorus") and reinventing Homeric and Hesiodic tales by focusing less on the central thrust of their narratives than on secondary details within them. In "The Death of Geryon," for example, the emphasis is placed on the delicate simile of the head and poppy, a rendering that shifts a reader's sympathies from Heracles (the slayer) to Geryon (the monster: "six-handed and six-footed and with wings"). Sadly, few fragments of Stesichorus' work survive, for he was considered one of the "nine great Greek lyric poets," Longinus even ranking him with Homer. Willis Barnstone provides this passage from Ammianus Marcellinus, the last of the great Roman historians: "There is a story that while Socrates was in prison, awaiting his death, he heard a man sing skillfully a song by the lyric poet [Stesichorus], and begged him to teach it to him before it was too late, and when the musician asked why, Socrates replied, 'I want to die knowing one thing more.'"

IBYCUS

"Vigil"
A disciple of Stesichorus, Ibycus combined the narrative refinements of the choral ode, as practiced by his mentor, with the more personal approaches of poets like Alcaeus and Sappho. The latter's influence may be seen here in a metaphor that recalls her description of erotic passion as "a headland wind thrashing out a leafed-out stand of oaks." To the ancients, Cydonian quince trees were a familiar emblem for the awakening of love, and it's just such symbolic representations that Ibycus juxtaposes with raw, unidealized experience. A reader may be interested to know that, as C. M. Bowra has noted, Ibycus "is the first Greek poet to say that the Morning and the Evening Star are the same, and this discovery, already made in Babylon, was first popularized by Pythagoras."

"The Winged Spirit's Afterthought"
Ibycus had a great love for birds, though more so than his peers with similar interests—and long before Aristotle's *Historia Animalium*—he depicted them in the particulars of their natural state. This love proved providential, as a number of

ancient sources record the following story. Traveling one day through a remote part of Samos, Ibycus was attacked and killed by a band of robbers. As he lay dying, he pointed to a flock of cranes overhead and declared that one day they'd avenge him. Some time afterward, as the robbers were entering a coastal city, one of them noticed some passing cranes and shouted to the others, "There are the avengers of Ibycus!" His cry drew the attention of people around him, and they in turn reported him to the authorities. The robbers were subsequently arrested and executed, and from this episode arose the expression "the cranes of Ibycus."

ANACREON

"Artemon and the Fates"
The public punishments referred to were meted out to buyers and sellers caught double-dealing in the marketplace.

"Jealousy"
As a possible source for this poem, several ancient writers report that, in a violent rage, Polycrates, a rival in love to Anacreon, cut off his beloved's hair. My text conflates the report with the poem.

XENOPHANES

During the Persian siege of his country, the twenty-five-year-old Xenophanes left his home to wander through Greece for the next sixty-seven years. A deeply philosophical poet and a fierce Skeptic, he expressed himself through parody and satire, a biting humor he was famous for directing at the theology of Hesiod and Homer as well as the views of Thales and Pythagoras. Aristotle notes that at one time Parmenides may have been Xenophanes' pupil, and certainly they shared similar ideas.

"The Image of God"
As one might gather from these fragments, Xenophanes rejected any claim for an anthropomorphic polytheism, believing instead in a single, transcendent, incorporeal spirit.

"Pythagoras"
Pythagoras was a contemporary of Xenophanes, and this poem makes light of the former's belief in the transmigration of souls.

"Prelude to a Conversation"
We may infer that the last question is meant to recall the year the Persians invaded Xenophanes' homeland.

"On Nature"
Section 5 recalls Homer's comparison (*The Iliad*, 11.27) of Agamemnon's shield to a rainbow.

SIMONIDES

Although sometimes cited as the first poet to associate poetry with "meanness of disposition"—and the first to write it for pay—Simonides was revered throughout Greece for his wit, his wise counsel, and his poetry. Noted for their emotional power (the proverbial expression "sadder than the tears of Simonides" suggests something of that power) and their highly refined details, his poems spoke directly to the Greek character and ideals; and, more important, they did so in a way that crossed political divisions between city-states. The first of Greece's national poets, he lived to the age of ninety and was said to possess a remarkable memory. Indeed, he originated the art of mnemonics, a system of associating one thing with another to better affix it in the mind.

"On Beauty"
Simonides' pessimistic side is often countered by an equally deep-seated belief in the nature of good and the beauty of art. Accordingly, he valued human conduct by the measures of virtue and imagination. This poem is a recasting of a passage from Hesiod: "But in front of Virtue have the deathless gods set sweat; long is the way thereto and steep and rough at first. But when a man has reached the summit, then it is easy, despite all its hardness."

"On Poetry and Painting"
I have combined two separate fragments (which may have appeared in poems, though we have them only in paraphrase), the first quoted by Michael Psellus in *The Function of Daemons,* the second by Plutarch in *The Glory of Athens.* Both are remarkable for the aesthetic issues they raise, for they were uttered in a culture that possessed no single word for art but regarded each art as yet another repository of wisdom. To associate poetry and painting this way was to identify a new aesthetic purpose, one whose success is determined not by its truth-telling properties but by the vividness and credulity with which it's registered on the eye. This elevates the "image" in poetry to a level of significance comparable to that in the visual arts, and it provides the West with one of its earliest intuitions of an "art for art's sake" aesthetic. Radical as this was, the future soon rose to its occasion. In *On the Sublime,* Longinus would define poetic inspiration as that state of mind wherein "you think you see what you describe, and you place it before the eyes of your hearers." Leonardo would observe in *Paragone* that "Painting is poetry which is seen and not heard, and

poetry is a painting which is heard and not seen." Shakespeare would articulate a similar preference through the guise of Henry V: "Think, when we talk of horses, that you see them / Printing their proud hoofs in the receiving earth." And Ruskin would elevate the visual image to the status of a religious paradigm: "The greatest thing a human soul ever does in this world is to see something, and tell what it saw in a plain way. Hundreds of people can talk for one who can think, but thousands can think for one who can see."

"Halcyon Days"

Aristotle cites this poem in a passage from *Historia Animalium*: "The halcyon nests about the time of the winter-solstice, and that is why, when the weather is fine at that time of year we call the days 'halcyon days,' being seven before and seven after the shortest day of the year."

"Danaë and Perseus Adrift"

Danaë was the daughter of the Argos king Acrisius. Having heard from an oracle that his daughter's son would kill him, Acrisius had Danaë locked away in a bronze cell. Still, driven by his desire for her, Zeus managed to penetrate the cell in a shower of gold, which led to the birth of Perseus. When her father learned of the birth, he locked mother and son in a brass-ribbed chest and set them adrift on the sea. At the end of the poem, Danaë addresses her prayer to Zeus in the hope that he might intercede in the fate of his own son.

"Dragonfly"

As was common among the early Greeks, Simonides believed that at any moment death and disaster might suddenly strike, and that one must always be prepared for their coming. His poems share with Pindar a sense of the wholly undiscriminating, wholly unpredictable nature of death. The appeal of this poem lies, of course, in the rightness of the image of the dragonfly, in its ability to capture on the wing, as it were, that extraordinary sense of the haphazard movements of fate.

PINDAR

"The Other World"

One of the greatest and most influential of the early Greek poets, Pindar composed in nearly all the choral genres, though he's principally known for his odes, a form that requires its own accounting. Nevertheless, because it stands on its own as a lyric poem (in the modern sense), I have taken the liberty of excerpting this passage from the last verse of his greatest ode, "Pythian VIII." Among the most celebrated lines in classical literature, they speak of the poet's profound sympathy for the idea that, lying behind the dreariness of mortal life, there exists an eternal world, a world lit by what he calls "the clear light of the mellisonant Graces."

CORINNA

Three surviving papyrus fragments written in Boeotian dialect suggest that Corinna lived in the third century B.C., though Plutarch reports that she was a mentor of Pindar's (fifth century B.C.), and legend has it that she defeated her famous pupil five times in poetry contests.

"The Contest of Two Mountains"
The two Boeotian mountains are Cithaeron and Helicon. Cithaeron is the second singer in the contest, and her song recalls certain details from Zeus's childhood. Rescued by his mother, Rhea, Zeus was hidden away in a cave in Crete to protect him from his jealous father, Cronos; Rhea accomplished this feat by substituting a stone for the son Cronos came to devour.

PRAXILLA

"Adonis in the Underworld"
Praxilla's reputation as a poet suffered from responses typical of attitudes toward women artists. This poem in particular drew such ridicule that the rhetorician Zenobius included in his *Proverbs* a phrase used for mocking fools, "Sillier than Praxilla's Adonis." The basis for his comment was the fact that Praxilla had elevated cucumbers to a level comparable in value to the sun: "as anyone who sets cucumbers beside the sun could only be called ridiculous." Not only does that comment seem strangely literal minded, but it also overlooks, as Josephine Balmer's *Classical Women Poets* points out, the fact that "a cucumber would seem an ideal emblem for any male fertility god. Praxilla is also punning here on the Greek for cucumber, *sikyos*, and the name of her native city, Sicyon." Like Sappho before her, Praxilla's reverence for the simple, commonplace pleasures of the world, for the small and humbly tendered, marks a sympathy that lies at the heart of the lyric poem. Perhaps the very fact that she set such things as cucumbers alongside the sun speaks of the depth to which she embraced the character of this new sensibility. Six centuries later, the poet Antipater of Thessalonica would declare Praxilla one of the earthly muses.

PLATO

It is traditionally recognized that, despite Plato's well-known philosophical qualms about the place of poetry within the Republic—"the honeyed muse," he cautioned, would make "pleasure and pain . . . the rulers in our State"—the great Athenian philosopher wrote poetry in his youth. And indeed, the small group of poems attributed to him reflects the same gifts for clarity, precision and nuance that characterize his prose.

"Aster I & II"

Aster (the name means "star") was a youth whom Plato is said to have loved, a youth, apparently, with an interest in astrology. No less an admirer than Shelley believed the second of these poems the most perfect of the early Greek lyrics; and indeed his own translation serves as the epigraph for *Adonais,* his great elegy for Keats.

"Hand-Carved Stone"

My translation combines two nearly identical poems, one by Plato and the other by King Polemo (of Pontus, first century B.C.), which appear side by side in *The Greek Anthology.*

ANONYMOUS

"Four Riddles, Two Enigmas"

Answers: (1) smoke (2) double flute (the oarsmen are the fingers) (3) artichoke (the last line refers to the core of the artichoke, which is its seed) (4) sleep (5) silence (6) day and night.

HELLENISTIC PERIOD (c. 323–31 B.C.)

ANONYMOUS

"Invitation to Oblivion"

W. R. Paton provides the following footnote: "Mackail compares the paradox in Plato's *Euthydemus* that it is impossible to learn what one does not know already, and hence impossible to learn at all."

ASCLEPIADES

"Love's Third Burden"

The last four lines, addressed to Zeus as the god of weather, are most likely meant to beg his mercy by recalling how, in his desire for Danaë, he was once overpowered by love as well. (See note on Simonides' "Danaë and Perseus Adrift.")

"Eros: An Attestation"

See note on Simonides' "Danaë and Perseus Adrift."

"The Waistband of Hermione"

The notion of a prior claim stitched into a piece of clothing will show up again in Petrarch's *Rime* 190 (fourteenth century), in Giovanni Antonio Romanello's imitation of that poem, "*Una cerva gentil*" (fifteenth century), and again in Thomas Wyatt's masterful "Whoso List to Hunt" (sixteenth century). While scholars debate whether Wyatt's poem imitates Romanello's or Petrarch's, I'm unaware of a connection being made to Asclepiades.

PHILETAS

Scholars remain uncertain if this Philetas (of Samos) is the same Philetas of Kos who served as the tutor for Theocritus, though Propertius and Ovid refer to them interchangeably.

ANYTE

Only twenty-one of Anyte's poems survive, all of them occasional insomuch as they served as inscriptions for both sepulchral and dedicatory stones. Some sources devalue her work for its domestic limitations—"On a Catalana Cock," for example, reveals her penchant for elegies to household pets—while others suggest that it quietly colludes with the patriarchal tradition by honoring such subjects as physical bravery and soldiers slain in battle. But neither estimation, to my mind, fully accounts for her real gift, her ability to conjure up scenes and experiences from the world around her, a gift that made a strong impression on no less a figure than Theocritus, the so-called founder of pastoral poetry.

"The Dwelling Place of Cypris"

Cypris is another name for Aphrodite.

ERINNA

Though sources vary, we have reason to believe that Erinna was a contemporary of Asclepiades (third century B.C.), who wrote a poem called "On Erinna (Inscribed on a Volume of Her Poems)." From his poem we learn that she died at the age of nineteen, and that, after her death, he may have edited her poems: "These are the poems of Erinna, / Hardly great in size, her dead at nineteen, / But far greater than many twice her age." Only three of her poems survive, plus another sixty or so lines from a long poem, *The Distaff*. In that poem Erinna recounts childhood experiences with her friend Baucis, who also died at a very young age, and whose death "Epitaph on a Bride's Tomb" commemorates.

"Epitaph on a Bride's Tomb"

In ancient Greece the wedding ceremony generally occurred in three stages, the second involving a procession in which the bride traveled from the house of her father to the house of her husband. A torch preceded the bride, and along the way songs were sung invoking the marriage god, Hymen. The name for these songs was hymeneals.

LEONIDAS OF TARENTUM

"Cicada"

In Plato's *Phaedrus,* Socrates provides an evolutionary history of the cicada: "It is said that they were once human beings in an age before the Muses. And when the Muses came and song appeared it seems the cicadas were so ravished with delight that, singing always, they never took thought of eating and drinking, until at last, without themselves noticing it, they died. It is from these men that the cicada species derives; as a special gift from the Muses, they require no nourishment, but from the hour of their birth they are always singing, and never eating or drinking, until they die; and when they die they go and inform the Muses in heaven which of us honors which of them. Those who have honored [one goddess or another] . . . they make even more dear to her by their report of them."

ANTIPATER OF SIDON

"The Bidding of the Harbor God"

As was often the case with seasonal and ceremonial poems of the period, similar versions with a shared stock of images—in this case, swallows nesting, meadows in bloom, hawsers being loosed, etc.—were composed by various poets.

MELEAGER

An accomplished and prolific poet, Meleager was admired for his technical invention, his stylistic virtuosity, and his ability to recast old forms and subjects in fresh and lively new ways. He compiled, if not the first anthology (from the Greek word for "flower gathering"), at least the first authoritative critical anthology of poetry. More than a thousand years later, *The Garland of Meleager* would become the principal source for *The Greek Anthology.*

"Praise Song"

The reference to bees streaming from the rotting carcasses of oxen is to be taken literally. As we learn from Book IV of Virgil's *Georgics,* the ancients believed that, by spontaneous generation, bees arose from the flesh of slaughtered cattle; we also learn that honey fell in the form of dew from heaven. It's within that disquisition on bees that Virgil enfolded the narrative of Orpheus' loss and failed attempt to recover Eurydice.

"To a Mosquito"
The rewards mentioned in the closing lines are emblems of power traditionally associated with Heracles.

ROMAN PERIOD (C. 31 B.C.–A.D. 500)

PHILODEMUS THE EPICUREAN

A fellow student of Cicero, Philodemus studied in Athens with the Epicurean philosopher Zeno. He later moved to Italy to assume a post at the Epicurean school in Naples, where, among other noteworthy students, he taught both Virgil and Horace. A model of intellectual inclusiveness, the Epicurean school welcomed men and women of all classes and required no fees, accepting only what each was willing to pay.

"O"
Paradoxically enough, since the woman here is reduced to a list of anatomical parts, the end of the poem wrestles with a cultural bias that viewed uneducated Italian women as unworthy attachments for educated Greek men. Perseus, the "Argive hero" of the last three lines, flew to the edge of the world (believed to be somewhere in North Africa) and there beheaded the snake-haired Medusa. On his return, Perseus passed through a kingdom in Ethiopia where Andromeda, daughter of King Cepheus and Cassiopeia, was being offered in sacrifice to appease a monster who threatened to ravage their land. On condition that he be allowed to marry the princess, Perseus fought and killed the beast. A northern constellation, Andromeda is located directly south of Cassiopeia and Perseus.

ANTIPATER OF THESSALONICA

"Water Drinkers"
This poem plays off the proverb "I hate a lively sidekick with a good memory." The morning setting of the Pleiades marked the end of the sailing season and the beginning of stormy weather.

PHILIP

Philip of Thessalonica is the anthologist of *The Garland of Philip* (A.D. 40), from which much of *The Greek Anthology* is drawn.

APOLLONIDES

"The Fates"
A more graphic version of a similar incident may be found in Virgil's *Georgics* (3.368–75).

BASSUS

"The Dream of Peace"
The Spartan soldiers referred to are those killed in the battle of Thermopylae.

LEONIDAS OF ALEXANDRIA
Renowned for his cleverness and taste for puzzles, Leonidas had forty poems included in *The Greek Anthology*. Of those, thirty were *isopsepha,* a now-extinct verse form wherein the sum of letters in each couplet adds up to the same number. Though I haven't attempted to reproduce the form, "Oxen" was composed in that measure.

AMMIANUS

"Days"
While the harrowing torments at the end of this poem are largely metaphorical, W. R. Paton points out that they also have a basis in symptoms common to particular (and often fatal) diseases of the day: i.e., tuberculosis, influenza, edema.

MESOMEDES

"The Invention of Glass"
The quarried stone is apparently some form of silica.

STRATO
The poems of Strato included here derive from Book XII of *The Greek Anthology,* a book entitled *Musa Paedika* (literally, "Pederasty Poems") compiled by Strato at the court of Hadrian in the second century A.D. Scholars are uncertain if, originally, Strato merely published a collection of his own poems, or if indeed the first publication was this anthology. Composed by some of the greatest poets in the Greek language, almost all the verses deal with some aspect of homosexual love for boys (though some heterosexual love poems are included as well). Whatever its evolution, the collection comes down to us in its anthology form and, as one might expect, it has been met with the full gamut of responses, from outrage and censorship to admiration and homage. It's worth remembering that the Greeks found nothing unusual in such relations—

indeed, they were considered quite fashionable in their day—and that the poems reflect the bracing openness of the period. For a spirited translation of the entire book, see Daryl Hine's *Puerilities: Erotic Epigrams of The Greek Anthology* (Princeton University Press, 2001).

PALLADAS

For most of his life, Palladas taught ancient (that is, pagan) literature in Alexandria, but with the violent advent of Christianity and the new antipagan laws, he lost his job late in life, sold his books, and finished out his years writing poetry.

RUFINUS

It is believed that Rufinus compiled an anthology of erotic verses, in which he included a large selection of his own. Certainly the erotic was a recurrent, perhaps even obsessive, subject in his work.

LICYMNIUS, SATYRUS, EVODUS, GLYCON

"A Garland from the Roman Empire"
(*River Acheron*)
This poem combines two fragments preserved in a passage from Porphyrius' *On the Styx* regarding the suitability of names given to rivers supposed to flow through hell. Acheron derives from the Greek word for "pains."
(*Echo*)
The ancients were particularly interested in the echo as both an earthly phenomenon and (though they'd hardly have distinguished between the two) as the nymph whose love for Narcissus led her to pine away until nothing remained but her voice. Hearing an echo, Echo would appear in the mind's eye of the ancient Greek.

EARLY BYZANTINE PERIOD (C. A.D. 500–600)

CHRISTODORUS

Christodorus of Thebes composed some seventy-five poems to describe the bronze statues in Zeuxippos, a renowned and apparently lavish Byzantine gymnasium. The gymnasium was destroyed by fire not long after he finished his project and, while many of his verses are overwritten and repetitive, at times they do—to use one of their author's oft-repeated shibboleths—"bring their subjects to life."

SELECTED BIBLIOGRAPHY

PRIMARY SOURCES

Bowra, C. M. *Greek Lyric Poetry: From Alcman to Simonides.* London: Oxford University Press, 1961.

———. *The Odes of Pindar.* New York, NY: Penguin Books, 1985.

———. *Pindari Carmina.* London: Oxford University Press, 1935.

Campbell, David A. *Greek Lyric I.* Cambridge, MA: Harvard University Press, 1994.

———. *Greek Lyric II.* Cambridge, MA: Harvard University Press, 1988.

———. *Greek Lyric III.* Cambridge, MA: Harvard University Press, 1991.

———. *Greek Lyric IV.* Cambridge, MA: Harvard University Press, 1992.

———. *Greek Lyric V.* Cambridge, MA: Harvard University Press, 1993.

Carne-Ross, D. S. *Pindar.* New Haven and London: Yale University Press, 1985.

Diehl, E. *Anthologia Lyrica Graeca: Fasc. 1, Poetae Elegiaci–Fasc. 3, Iamborum Scriptores.* Leipzig: Teubner, 1954.

Easterling, P. E., and B. M. W. Knox, eds. *The Cambridge History of Classical Literature, Volume I, Part I: Early Greek Poetry.* Cambridge, England: Cambridge University Press, 1989.

Edmonds, J. M. *Elegy and Iambus I.* Cambridge, MA: Harvard University Press, 1968.

———. *Elegy and Iambus II.* Cambridge, MA: Harvard University Press, 1968.

———. *Lyra Graeca I.* Cambridge, MA: Harvard University Press, 1922.

———. *Lyra Graeca II.* Cambridge, MA: Harvard University Press, 1964.

———. *Lyra Graeca III.* Cambridge, MA: Harvard University Press, 1967.

Gerber, Douglas E. *Greek Elegiac Poetry.* Cambridge, MA: Harvard University Press, 1999.

———. *Greek Iambic Poetry.* Cambridge, MA: Harvard University Press, 1999.

Gow, A. S. F., and D. L. Page. *The Garland of Philip I: Text and Translation*. Cambridge, England: Cambridge University Press, 1968.

———. *The Garland of Philip II: Commentary and Indexes*. Cambridge, England: Cambridge University Press, 1968.

———. *The Greek Anthology I: Text and Translation*. Cambridge, England: Cambridge University Press, 1965.

———. *The Greek Anthology II: Commentary and Indexes*. Cambridge, England: Cambridge University Press, 1965.

Mulroy, David. *Early Greek Lyric Poetry*. Ann Arbor, MI: University of Michigan Press, 1992.

Page, D. L. *Alcman: The Partheneion*. London: Oxford University Press, 1951.

———. *Further Greek Epigrams*. Cambridge, England: Cambridge University Press, 1981.

———. *Poetae Melici Graeci*. London: Oxford University Press, 1962.

———. *Sappho and Alcaeus*. London: Oxford University Press, 1955.

———. *Supplementum Lyricis Graecis*. London: Oxford University Press, 1974.

Paton, W. R. *The Greek Anthology I*. 1916. Reprint, Cambridge, MA: Harvard University Press, 1999.

———. *The Greek Anthology II*. 1917. Reprint, Cambridge, MA: Harvard University Press, 2000.

———. *The Greek Anthology III*. 1917. Reprint, Cambridge, MA: Harvard University Press, 1998.

———. *The Greek Anthology IV*. 1918. Reprint, Cambridge, MA: Harvard University Press, 1999.

———. *The Greek Anthology V*. 1918. Reprint, Cambridge, MA: Harvard University Press, 1999.

SELECTED TRANSLATIONS

Balmer, Josephine. *Classical Women Poets*. Newcastle upon Tyne, England: Bloodaxe Books Ltd., 1996.

Barnard, Mary. *Sappho*. Berkeley, CA: University of California Press, 1966.

Barnstone, Willis. *Sappho and the Greek Lyric Poets*. New York, NY: Schocken Books, 1988.

Bing, Peter, and Rip Cohen. *Games of Venus: An Anthology of Greek and Roman Erotic Verse from Sappho to Ovid*. New York, NY: Routledge, 1991.

Carson, Anne. *If Not, Winter: Fragments of Sappho*. New York, NY: Alfred A. Knopf, 2002.

Chandler, Robert. *Sappho*. London: J. M. Dent, 1998.

Fitts, Dudley. *Poems from the Greek Anthology*. New York, NY: New Directions, 1956.

Hine, Daryl. *Puerilities: Erotic Epigrams of The Greek Anthology*. Princeton, NJ: Princeton University Press, 2001.

Jay, Peter. *The Greek Anthology: And Other Ancient Greek Epigrams*. New York, NY: Penguin Books, 1981.

Lattimore, Richmond. *Greek Lyrics*. Chicago, IL: University of Chicago Press, 1971.

Leslie, Shane. *The Greek Anthology*. London: Ernst Benn Limited, 1929.

Mills, Barriss. *The Soldier and the Lady: Poems of Archilochos and Sappho*. New Rochelle, NY: The Elizabeth Press, 1975.

Poole, Adrian, and Jeremy Maule. *The Oxford Book of Classical Verse in Translation*. London: Oxford University Press, 1995.

Rayor, Diane J. *Sappho's Lyre: Archaic Lyric and Women Poets of Ancient Greece*. Berkeley, CA: University of California Press, 1991.

Rexroth, Kenneth. *Poems from the Greek Anthology*. Ann Arbor, MI: University of Michigan Press, 1999.

Reynolds, Margaret. *The Sappho Companion*. New York, NY: Palgrave, 2000.

Roche, Paul. *The Love Songs of Sappho*. Amherst, NY: Prometheus Books, 1998.

Skelton, Robin. *Two Hundred Poems from the Greek Anthology*. Seattle, WA: University of Washington Press, 1971.

Washburn, Katharine, John S. Major, and Clifton Fadiman. *World Poetry: An Anthology of Verse from Antiquity to Our Time*. New York, NY: W. W. Norton & Company, Inc., 1998.

West, M. L. *Greek Lyric Poetry: The Poems and Fragments of the Greek Iambic, Elegiac, and Melic Poets (excluding Pindar and Bacchylides) down to 450 B.C.* Oxford, England: Clarendon Press, 1993.

INDEX OF POEMS AND SOURCES

Except where otherwise indicated, book and number references in the right-hand column (e.g., 5.237) refer to the standardized numbering found in the Loeb Classical Library's *The Greek Anthology,* W. R. Paton, 5 vols., Harvard University Press, 1998–2000. Other texts refer to book and/or page numbers in editions listed in the Primary Sources section of the Selected Bibliography.

INDEX OF AUTHORS, TITLES, AND FIRST LINES

Authors are indexed in **bold type**, first lines in roman, and titles in *italic*.